M I K

THE TORTOISE
AND THE HARE

**LEARNING TO RUN & WIN
THE RACES THAT MATTER** R E T O L D

High Tide Press

Published by High Tide Press, Inc.
101 Hempstead Place, Suite 1A, Joliet, IL 60433
hightidepress.org

The tortoise and the hare retold:
Learning to run and win the races that matter

Michael Mecozzi, Psy.D.

ISBN: 978-1-892696-79-3

Designed by Arjan van Woensel

Printed in the United States of America

DEDICATION

To my Dad who won in life. (Psalm 103:1-5)

TABLE OF CONTENTS

PREFACE

Our natural inclination is most always
to move more quickly than is useful.
— Kelly Wilson

When I was a kid, my parents bought me a cassette tape of Aesop's
fables. Since I've always enjoyed the underdog story, I subjected my
younger brother to repeated replays of "The Tortoise and the Hare." The
idea of a tortoise beating a hare in a race was as inconceivable as the
Chicago Cubs winning a World Series. Remarkably, the Cubs did win a
World Series, and the tortoise did defeat the hare, proving that almost
anything is possible.

The world around us has changed dramatically since Aesop wrote
"The Tortoise and the Hare." I recently read that we are exposed to as
much information in a day as people were exposed to in a lifetime 500
years ago! It's no wonder that we are anxious and stressed. What further
adds to our current challenges is that the information we hear and read
often promotes drama, fright and uncertainty.

In the context of this fast-paced, anxiety-driven world, "The Tortoise
and the Hare" seems even more relevant. The fable's lesson is understood to be, "Slow and steady wins the race," or "The race is not always
to the swift." In today's world, anything that idealizes a slow pace seems

outdated. However, there continues to be much wisdom to be found from this ancient fable. In the pages that follow, we will join the hare as he learns lessons from the tortoise on how to win in today's world, and specifically how to live a full and contented life. The tortoise begins by describing the wrong, destructive races we run, such as a "rat race"; he then discusses the right races to run and offers advice on how to run them with confidence and courage. Through their conversations, questions, answers and real-life demonstrations, the hare learns how to live successfully.

Although I believe this book to be relevant to most audiences, it is written with young adults in mind. They may be just graduating from high school, working at their first job, coming out of the military, preparing for college, or simply seeking a career that appeals to them. In my work as a psychologist, I have seen how challenging it is to be surrounded by seemingly endless choices. Young people are asked to figure out what they want to do in life, who they want to be, what their ideal job is and whom they should partner with. They are further warned to avoid any mistakes, lest they ruin their lives. This can be a heavy burden to bear. My goal in writing this book is to offer some ideas and insights that might give readers hope, direction and motivation.

Paradoxically, although what follows will likely help the reader to slow down, it's intentionally short and concise so that it can be read quickly. Thanks for taking the time to read *The Tortoise and the Hare Retold*. Now let's get on with the race!

A NOTE ABOUT THE SETTING

I have endeavored to create a setting that is playful, educational and inspiring. Of course, hares and tortoises don't hang out together, and it isn't at all likely that you'll see zebras and gazelles running around in a forest inhabited by Macaw parrots. But for the purpose of this book, I ask you to use your imagination and hold on to the idea that this forest is special—we might even say enchanted—a place where many different animals reside, where animals talk, and their lives reflect the everyday experiences that we humans can relate to: meaning, relationships, doubts, uncertainties, fears, joy and gratitude.

TORTOISE HOME

GRAVEL PATH

BLUE DIAMOND POND

DECIDUOUS FOREST

HARE HOME

SWAMP

TOWERING EVERGREEN

FINISH!

START

CHAPTER ONE

THE TORTOISE AND THE HARE

There was once a hare who lived in a very large forest. Hare did everything fast. He ran fast; he talked fast; and he ate fast. But the one thing he didn't do was plan fast; in fact, he barely ever planned; he just reacted.

In the same forest lived a tortoise. Everything Tortoise did, he did intentionally. He walked with purpose; he talked with purpose; and he planned before he acted. Tortoise had specific goals for his life, and he worked toward them one step at a time.

One thing Hare enjoyed was boasting about his speed. He never let a single animal in the forest forget that he was very, very fast. One day, Hare spotted Tortoise, who was taking a slow, relaxing walk on a path near his home. Hare sprinted in between the trees, enjoying the autumn breeze that swept across his fur. He was obviously enjoying himself.

"Hey, slowpoke!" Hare yelled as he got closer. Initially, Tortoise ignored him. Hare, however, didn't like being ignored, so he walked up to the tortoise and said loudly, "Hey, slowpoke. I'm talking to you!"

Although annoyed, Tortoise greeted him respectfully. "Hi, Hare. How are you?"

"Oh, I'm great. I'm great because I'm the fastest animal in the forest. How are you? I can't imagine you're too great since you're the slowest animal in the world," Hare teased rudely.

Tortoise paused, collected his thoughts, and replied, "You know what, Hare? We should have a race."

"What?! Did I hear you correctly?"

"You sure did. I challenge you to a race."

"You want to race a hare? A turtle race a hare? Ha!"

"I'm a tortoise, not a turtle," stated Tortoise. "And yes, I am challenging you to a race."

"Turtle, tortoise. Who cares? All the same thing. I accept your challenge. This is going to be the easiest race I've ever run." And Hare ran off laughing.

Tortoise knew he would have to make all the race preparations, so he spent the next few days contacting animals to help set up the race. He also announced it to all the other animals with the help of his trusty friend, the Macaw parrot. When he squawked, the animals couldn't help but listen!

Anticipation filled the air as race day approached. All the animals knew that the hare would win, but they were all rooting for the tortoise. They were tired of the hare's boasting, but none of them had the tortoise's courage to challenge him to a race.

Finally, the day of the race arrived. A huge crowd of animals gathered in a clearing around the starting line to watch the two contestants take off. Although the leaves were beginning to change colors, warmth filled the air. It was a perfect day for a race.

Zebra was, of course, selected as the race official because of his black and white stripes. He described the course to Tortoise, Hare and all the spectators. "You'll start by running on the path that goes through the middle of the forest. When you reach the Blue Diamond Pond, continue to your right. You'll run around the pond and then find a gravel path that the humans created. Take that path to the towering evergreen tree. Behind the evergreen tree, there is a dirt trail. Take that trail south, and it will bring you to the finish line. Any questions?"

Both Tortoise and Hare shook their heads. They had no questions.

"Okay, if there are no questions, I'll turn it over to the parrot." The large Macaw had agreed to whistle loudly to signal the beginning of the race. Everyone held their breath and then covered their ears when the Macaw signaled with a screech instead of a whistle.

The race began, and Hare jumped into the lead. He stopped at the Blue Diamond Pond and took a moment to admire his reflection. "Wow, my blue eyes match the color of this beautiful pond," he thought to himself. Hare turned to look behind him, but Tortoise was nowhere in sight! He continued to the towering evergreen tree. Still no sign of the tortoise! Hare had such a large lead that he decided to explore the forest for a while before finishing the race. After several minutes, he concluded that he had time for a quick nap since he was still well ahead of the tortoise. However, his short nap became a long one.

Meanwhile, Tortoise continued at his slow, steady pace. He also noticed his reflection at Blue Diamond Pond but did not stop.

He took a few deep breaths and told himself, "Just keep moving, Tortoise. Just keep moving." He looked ahead, but the hare was nowhere in sight. Even so, he kept moving, one step after another. His feet ached, and his shell seemed to grow heavier as the race continued. When he finally reached the towering evergreen tree, he had thoughts of quitting, but he kept going until he reached the dirt trail. He could see the finish line! As he approached, he heard the other animals cheering him on. When he crossed the finish line, the animals shouted, "You won! You won!"

"I won?" gasped the shocked tortoise.

"You won!" they shouted again.

At that very moment, Hare awoke from his nap. He sprinted to the finish line, but much to his dismay and disbelief, Tortoise was already there. The hare had lost the race to the tortoise.

CHAPTER TWO

RUNNING THE RIGHT RACES

The forest animals surrounded Tortoise to celebrate his victory. They were so happy that they would no longer have to deal with the hare's constant boasting. Tortoise laughed and talked for a while but soon decided to return home to be with his wife. The animals picked him up and carried him in a jubilant parade all the way to his home.

Tortoise was tired from his long race, but his efforts to rest were interrupted repeatedly by animals stopping by to congratulate him. There would be no extra sleep tonight.

The congratulatory visits finally ended as the afternoon turned to evening. However, when he was about to start preparing for bed, he heard a soft knock at the door. It was a faint knock, a knock that sounded timid, almost accidental. Tortoise was curious as the earlier knocks had been loud and unmistakable, matching each animal's excitement about his victory. He walked slowly to the door and opened it. To his surprise, it was Hare.

"Hey, Hare! I didn't expect you."

"Yeah, I know, Tortoise," he said somewhat uneasily. "Can I come in?"

"Sure, come on in. So, how are you?"

"Not so good. I just lost a race. To a tortoise." Hare managed a slight smile. "But you beat me fair and square. How are you?"

"I'm pretty tired. That race took a lot out of me. What brings you here?"

"I was hoping we could talk."

"And then I realized this: even if you had lost, you still would have been happy. You're clearly winning in life."

Tortoise moved back and motioned Hare toward a chair in the living room just inside the door. "Sure," he answered. "Here, have a seat in this chair. We can sit and relax a little. What do you want to talk about?"

Hare sat down, looking obviously uncomfortable. "I'm not sure how to say this. You know, it was quite embarrassing losing to a tortoise. I'll never hear the end of it. But, ummmm," Hare looked down at his feet, and hardly above a whisper said, "I'm sorry."

"Sorry?" Tortoise looked surprised. "What for?"

"Because I was mean to you. I teased you. I made fun of your lack of speed. I called you a turtle instead of a tortoise. But it turns out, the joke's on me."

Tortoise got up from his chair, leaned over and patted Hare gently on the shoulder. "I appreciate that, Hare. It really means a lot to me that you came all this way to apologize."

Hare paused, and then gathered his courage. "Well, there's actually one other reason I came over."

Tortoise sat down again and looked at his visitor inquisitively. "And what's that?" he asked.

"I wanted to know if you could help me."

"Help you?"

"Yes, help me."

"I guess I'm a little confused, Hare. How can I help you? Help you with what?"

"I used to feel sorry for you tortoises. You do everything so slowly, and you seem to have a boring life. But today, I realized something, and it wasn't only because I lost the race. When I crossed that finish line, I looked and saw how many friends you have, how many animals were rooting for you. Nobody rooted for me. No one wanted me to win. When I crossed the finish line, I was alone.

"And then I realized this: even if you had lost, you still would have been happy. You're clearly winning in life, and I'm beginning to realize that I'm losing in life. So will you teach me how to live a better life?"

Tortoise was humbled by Hare's request. "Wow, that means a lot, Hare. I never would have thought that you would want to learn from me. I'd be honored to help you learn how to live a more fulfilling life."

Hare's face brightened. "I'm ready. When do we start?"

"Well, you see, Hare, to live a better life you have to...."

"I know, I know," interrupted Hare. "I know what you're going to say. I've heard the fable before! To live a good life, you have to remember that 'Slow and steady wins the race,' right?"

Tortoise laughed out loud.

Hare stared in astonishment. "Why are you laughing?" he asked.

"We tortoises have modernized. Although "slow and steady" is still important, we've updated our slogan. No one likes to go slow anymore, not even tortoises."

Hare smiled. "That is a relief. You are right, no one wants to go slow, especially me. What's the new slogan?"

"Embrace the race."

"Embrace the race? What does that mean?"

"To live your best possible life, you have to run the right races. 'Embrace the race' means you identify the races that truly matter, and then you learn how to win them. But running these races doesn't mean you defeat other contestants."

> ## *"'Embrace the race' means you identify the races that truly matter, and then you learn how to win them."*

Hare thought for a few moments, looked up and asked, "What are the right races?"

"That's a great question. The right races are not a competition. They are races where you're growing, gaining in wisdom and helping others.

There are four races that seem especially important: Purpose, Love, Action, and Noticing the positive. These four races create the acronym PLAN. To win at life, you need to have a plan, and the PLAN is to run with Purpose, run with Love, run with Action and run with Positivity. But I'm getting a bit ahead of myself. Before you can run these four races, you have to understand that you might be running the wrong races."

Tortoise noticed Hare's even more puzzled look and continued. "Let me give you an example. It seems like you are running the rat race—no offense to our little friends! When you're running the rat race, you're searching for overnight success and fame. You want fortune and power. You want ease. You think you always have to win. Your life has exciting moments, but I bet they don't last. Then, when you feel afraid or disappointed, you run to the next project or big idea, only to have the pattern repeat itself.

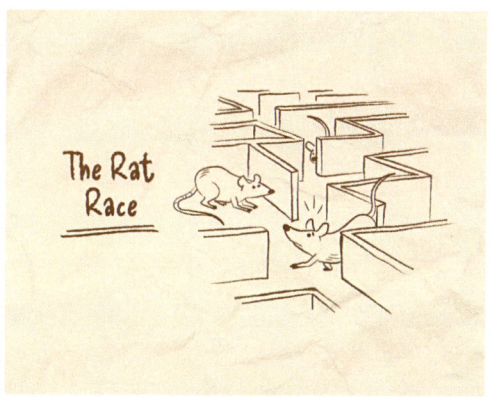

"I know this because I used to run the wrong races. Sometimes I still run the wrong races. But when I focus on the PLAN, I win more in life."

Hare reflected, "I guess I have been running the wrong races. And come to think of it, today hasn't been the only race I've lost. I feel like I'm losing in other areas of life as well." Hare paused before asking, "So how do I focus on the PLAN and start choosing the right races?"

Tortoise looked out his window. Dusk was approaching as the sun sank below the horizon in a sea of color. How grateful he was for the sunshine, for his friends, for today's race! His thoughts returned to Hare sitting across from him. "To start, we'll need to talk more about the races that we shouldn't run. But it's getting late, and my wife and I are leaving tomorrow for a two-week vacation. We're just going to the other side of the forest, but at the pace we move, it will take us about five days to get there and five days to get back home. So, if it's okay with you, could we pick this back up when we return?"

Hare pretended to be disappointed. "Oh no, I have to wait! Hares don't like waiting. But I guess I'll 'Embrace the race' and do my best! Okay, I will see you in two weeks. Have a good trip."

Hare stood up and exchanged good-byes with Tortoise. He walked out of the door thoughtfully, then hopped through the forest with an extra bounce in his step. Tortoise returned to his chair, took a deep breath, exhaled and thought to himself, "*A tortoise teaching a hare? What have I gotten myself into?*" He paused, took another deep breath and went to bed. He was excited about the opportunity to help his new friend live a better life.

CHAPTER THREE

THE RACE OF COMPARISON

The two weeks passed slowly for Hare. He did not like to wait! Even though daylight was growing shorter, the days seemed to grow longer and longer as he awaited Tortoise's return. Finally, it was time to meet. Hare woke up early, eager to start learning the lessons. He ran almost as fast as he had during the end of the race and was panting when he knocked on Tortoise's door as the sun slowly crept above the horizon.

While he waited for an answer, he realized that he couldn't remember the last time he had been up this early! He also wondered when in the past he had felt such anticipation. But as good as that felt, it scared him, too. He didn't want to experience another disappointment in his life. His thoughts were finally interrupted when Tortoise opened the door.

"Hi, friend!" Tortoise exclaimed as he welcomed Hare in with a wave.

"Would you like anything to drink?"

"How about a carrot cappuccino," Hare joked.

Tortoise smiled. "Oh, I see how this is going to be. Unfortunately, this isn't a coffee shop, and all I can offer you is a hot cup of coffee with sugar and cream or a cup of tea. On the positive side, I won't charge you $10 for the drink."

Hare chuckled and nodded. "Free coffee is good," he said.

Tortoise went to the kitchen and returned with Hare's coffee. He handed him the cup and pointed to two chairs in the living room. "Pick a chair and relax," he said.

Hare sat down in the same chair he had used two weeks ago, placing his cup on the small table that separated the two chairs. Tortoise sat across from him. As Hare got comfortable, he yawned. Though he tried hard to hide it, there was no masking the fact that he wasn't normally awake at such early hours.

"Am I boring you already?" asked Tortoise.

"Oh no, not at all. I'm sorry. I'm just not usually up this early."

"Yes, it is early," agreed Tortoise. Then he got out of his chair and brought Hare a pen and a notebook. "Here, my friend. Would you like a pen and paper in case you want to take some notes or jot down some questions? It might help you remember in the future."

Hare yawned again and nodded in agreement. "Wow, you think of everything."

Tortoise continued. "Like I mentioned a few weeks ago, before we talk about the right races to run, it's helpful to identify the wrong races we are running. These are races that we are taught will lead to winning in life, but they almost always come up short. Last time we met I mentioned that the rat race is one of the wrong races we run. When we're running the rat race, it's like we're doing things for no good reason.

It seems as though we are always competing for something we can never get enough of. It's like a daily grind, and we feel exhausted at the end of the day. But the rat race isn't the only wrong race we run. We're going to talk about five additional unhelpful races.

"The first is 'The Race of Comparison.'"

Hare scribbled the words in his notebook. "What's a race of comparison?" he asked.

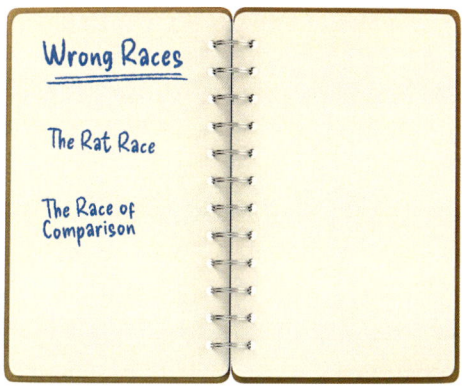

"It's probably the most common race. We are constantly comparing ourselves to others. We believe that life is a competition, and if we beat or defeat others, we are winning. We believe that if we have the better job, the better house, even the better family, then we beat everyone else and win."

"Yup. I know that race."

"We all do. And what's the problem with this race?"

"Well, as I learned not long ago, we don't always win." Hare smiled with some embarrassment.

"That's right. But let's say you had won our race. What would that have done for you?"

Hare thought for a moment. "Not much, I guess. I might have been excited for a few moments, but then I would have remembered that I should have beaten you. You are a tortoise after all. The excitement would have quickly faded away."

Tortoise nodded. "And that's the problem with the race of comparison: it steals our contentment and replaces it with constant striving. And, when we're constantly trying to be better than others, it can leave us feeling alone. We're so focused on defeating others that we don't take the time to build relationships and work together."

"It seems like we are always comparing ourselves to others. Why do we do that when it can cause us to be dissatisfied and alone?"

"The ability to make comparisons is actually very helpful. Humans are very good at making comparisons, and so are we. That's why they've been able to build large buildings, fly airplanes and even travel to outer space. Comparison allows us to learn, identify problems and solve them.

"And that's the problem with the race of comparison: it steals our contentment and replaces it with constant striving."

But it also allows us to find faults in ourselves. We look at the other animals, and it looks like the deer is sleeker, the squirrel more agile, the owl wiser and the gazelle faster. We attempt to deal with our deficits by comparing ourselves with others, thinking that if we defeat them, then we are good enough. But even if we do win, we can still be preoccupied with our deficits."

"That's how I feel," Hare observed sadly.

"And that's why the race of comparison is unhelpful. This race is supported by the idea that we win in life when we defeat others. That turns out to be a myth. Defeating others only provides temporary satisfaction. And for most animals, there is always another animal that is better than they are. But even if you're the undisputed champion, or as humans like to say, the G.O.A.T. (Greatest of All Time), if you don't spend time building relationships and appreciating what you have, being the champion can be a lonely, unsatisfying place to be."

"Well, what about competing with yourself? Is it helpful to compete with yourself?" asked Hare.

"It can be helpful to set goals for yourself, to strive to get better, and not be satisfied with where you are. But if we become preoccupied with always beating our previous achievements, it can still lead to an unsatisfying life because the win never lasts. We can always improve. We can always get better. But if our self-worth is based entirely on whether we are better than we previously were, then we're never able to experience contentment. We're constantly striving for something that can never be reached. It's important to constantly strive to improve, but it's equally important to celebrate what we have accomplished."

"Okay, you've convinced me that the race of comparison is a losing race. What's the next race I need to avoid?"

CHAPTER FOUR

THE RACE
OF WEALTH

"There is an assumption," Tortoise continued, "that we win in life when we have more, own more. We call this 'The Race of Wealth.'"

Hare picked up his pen and wrote the words in his notebook. "I think I know where you're going with this one," he said.

"What we own and how much we own," explained Tortoise, "can be used as a way to measure success. Our possessions and the money we have can quickly become the finish line. We believe that once we have a certain amount of money or a certain number or type of possessions, we win. Humans especially get trapped in the race of wealth."

Hare scratched his head and frowned. "So why is this the wrong race? Working hard to get more doesn't seem like a bad thing."

"The problem of racing for more is that there is always more to race for. We cross one finish line, and as soon as we cross that line, there's something else we think we need or should have. We can always have more money and more possessions. When we are always racing for more, we are never satisfied."

> ## *"When we are always racing for more, we are never satisfied."*

Hare considered some of his own choices. "Yeah, I've always been running after the carrot on the stick—pun intended!" They both laughed. "But even when I get the carrot," he confessed, "it never seems like it's satisfying or enough."

Tortoise nodded. "And that's the second reason why this race is an unhelpful one. Money, possessions and things ultimately don't satisfy. They may help us feel comfortable, but not contented, since they don't fulfill our needs for companionship and purpose. Humans like to say, 'You can't buy happiness.' We tortoises like to say, 'You can't buy meaning and purpose.' Money can offer a sense of security, but possessions don't provide meaning in your life."

"I like that. 'You can't buy meaning and purpose.'"

"Yes, I like it, too. Unfortunately, it is so easy to start running after more things. At times I find myself thinking, *'If I just had the newest phone,'* or *'if I could just afford a nicer place to live, then I would be happy.'* These thoughts are enticing, but when we listen to them too closely, they lead us to run a race that can't be won."

"So, is it wrong to want things?"

"No. It's natural to want. As a hare, I'm sure you want to eat carrots, and I'm sure you also want to wear karats." They both chuckled at Tortoise's play on words.

"Yes, I want them both. The orange ones are a little easier to come by than the gold ones though."

Tortoise smiled. "What's important," he said, "is not confusing our wants with our needs."

"How do we do that?" asked Hare.

"Well, you might want karats, but you don't actually need them. When we confuse our wants with our needs, we start running the race of wealth, which is fueled by the thought that if we have everything we want, then we win in life."

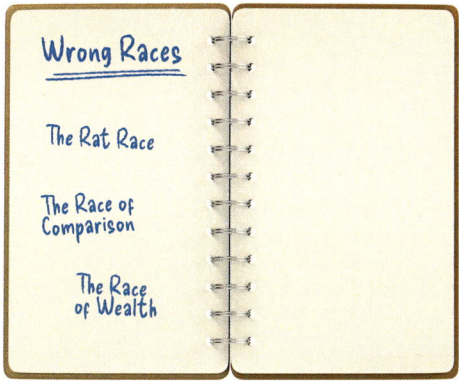

Hare nodded his head in agreement. "That makes sense to me. It's so easy to look around at others, see what they have and believe I need to have what they have."

"It sure is," Tortoise agreed. "In fact, the race of comparison and the race of wealth can fuel one another. It seems like other animals have more than we do, and it seems like other animals are happier than we are. Logically, we conclude that if we could just have what they have, then we would be happy. The problem is, the race of comparison and the race of wealth can only provide temporary feelings of happiness, but they eventually lead to dissatisfaction."

"Okay. So, what's the next unhelpful race we run?"

CHAPTER FIVE

THE RACE
OF EASE

Tortoise shifted in his chair and took a drink of coffee. "Several years back humans created an advertisement for a particular store. In it, they showed a large red button with the word 'Easy' on it. The ad concluded that shopping at the store was like pressing an easy button, and it highlights the next unhelpful race we run, 'The Race of Ease.'"

Hare added the third race to his list. "This one seems pretty self-explanatory, but tell me about it."

Tortoise paused and then observed. "We like ease, and we like activities that take little effort. If given a choice, we will almost always choose the easy way over the hard way. When you walked to my house today, did you take the long path around the forest, or did you take the short path that cuts through it?"

"The shorter path, of course."

"Why?"

"Because it's easier."

"Exactly. We like it when things are easy and comfortable. So we start running the race of ease and look to create more and more comfort in our life."

"I do like being comfortable." Hare slouched a bit in his chair and grinned.

"And you're not alone. Those humans even have things they sit in called Laz-y-boys!"

"Yeah, I've heard of those. I've always wanted to try one," Hare said wistfully. "So why is this race unhelpful?"

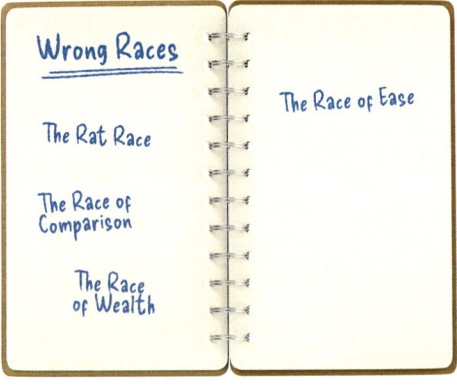

"No one enjoys doing things that make them uncomfortable. It's very common to keep putting things off that need to be done. Humans have a word for this. It's called procrastination."

Hare nodded. "Yes, I've heard of that word. I'm pretty good at putting things off, too."

"Me, too," said Tortoise. "But when we put things off and choose the easy way, we can miss out on important opportunities. Let's take our race from a couple of weeks ago."

"Do we have to?" Hare moaned comically and both animals laughed.

"Racing you made me *very* uncomfortable," Tortoise confessed. "It could have been an extremely embarrassing experience for me. But I want to be able to do tough things that help me grow. I want to stretch myself. And I knew that racing you would be quite the challenge. But, if I had chosen the easy way, I would never have asked to race you; I would never have won; and we wouldn't be talking right now."

"So, there's a cost to choosing the easy way."

―――――

"When we put things off and choose the easy way, we can miss out on important opportunities."

―――――

"Yes, there is. That cost is lack of growth. We don't grow. We don't do what matters most to us. And we don't change. Almost any change, even if it's a positive change, creates discomfort. If our focus is on running the race of ease, we will always stay the same. Actually, it's quite ironic. The word 'comfort' comes from two Latin words: *com* meaning 'with' and *fort* meaning 'strength.' Comfort literally means 'with strength.'"

"That's cool!" exclaimed Hare.

"So instead of living the race of ease and comfort, we want to live the literal definition of comfort: *with strength*."

"So how do I live with strength instead of living for ease?"

"Well," Tortoise answered, "I'm getting a little ahead of myself again. Before we get to that, we've got two more races to explore. Are you ready for the next one?"

"Let's do it!" said Hare enthusiastically.

CHAPTER SIX

THE RACE
OF FAME

Another common unhelpful belief is that we only win in life when lots
of animals are aware that we are winning. This belief leads to 'The Race
of Fame.'"

Hare wrote down the race. "All right. Tell me more. What's this one
all about?"

Tortoise looked at Hare quizzically and asked, "Have you ever felt that
in order to win in life you need to be important?"

Hare reddened all the way to the tip of his nose and looked at the
floor. "Yeah. I guess that's where my boasting came from. I liked being
the fastest animal in the forest. That's one of the reasons I raced you. I
wanted to win easily and be the talk of the forest."

"Yup. We like to be noticed, and that's not a bad thing," Tortoise commented gently. "But when the purpose of life is about being noticed and famous, it's another set-up for failure."

"Why?"

"First, we can't control what others are going to think about us. Animals', and from what I understand, humans' opinions are ever changing. One moment you are a hero, and the next you're not."

"Yeah, and sometimes the fame you get you don't want," Hare added uncomfortably. "I'm quite famous now, famous for being the only hare that's ever lost a race to a tortoise."

"The spotlight can be nice, but sometimes it can be hot."

"It sure can!"

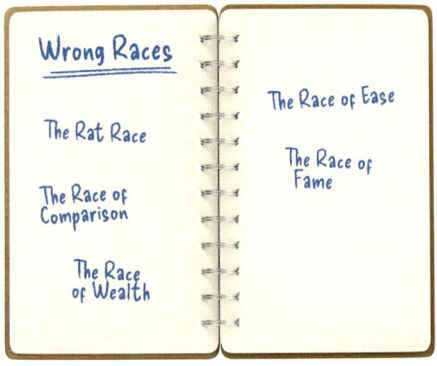

Tortoise paused for a moment. "Ultimately," he said thoughtfully, "fame deceives. It tells us that if others recognize us, then we are worthwhile. But acceptance from others and acceptance of ourselves doesn't come from being recognized; acceptance comes from being open and vulnerable. And we can only be truly known in the context of meaningful, connected relationships."

"So, it's not about the number of likes on social media?"

"No. I'm glad that we animals don't have social media. From what I understand, social media can cause a lot of stress and comparison. It's nice to be noticed, but it's meaningful to be known."

"Okay," replied Hare with a tinge of impatience in his voice. "Then how can we be known?"

> *" And we can only be truly known in the context of meaningful, connected relationships."*

Tortoise laughed. "I'm sorry I keep saying this, but we're not quite there yet. However, I promise you, we will talk about that later. There's just one more race to review, and then we will CHOOSE the PLAN. We are able to be known when we CHOOSE the PLAN."

Hare sighed as playfully as he could. "Remember I'm a hare. I don't like all this waiting."

"I know. But 'slow and steady wins the race.'"

"Hey, I thought you changed your slogan."

"We did. But we still use 'slow and steady wins the race' when it's convenient."

"Okay. Well, let's get to the last race so we can CHOOSE the PLAN," Hare stated emphatically.

CHAPTER SEVEN

THE RACE OF IMPULSIVITY

"Let's do it!" agreed Tortoise and took a sip of coffee. "I want to clear up a possible misconception you may have about tortoises. We don't believe that it's a bad thing to go fast. Sometimes in life, you have to go fast to win. But if you're running fast in the wrong direction, then it's unhelpful to go fast. And that leads to the final race, 'The Race of Impulsivity.'"

Hare picked up his pen and wrote, "The Race of Impulsivity." "Now tell me about this one," he said.

Tortoise obliged him promptly. "We are inundated with choices and information. And sometimes we are so overwhelmed by all the information that we make impulsive decisions. We don't take the time to consider our best options. We are distracted by all of the information, and we make a quick choice so we don't have to think about the information anymore. But the impulsive choices we make today are often tomorrow's problems."

"Do you have an example?"

"Okay, consider this example that I understand many teenagers experience. The teen is thinking about where to go to college or what job opportunities to pursue.

He has hundreds of options and is worried that he's going to make the wrong choice. It feels like there are too many things to consider. So instead of considering his most important priorities related to the quality of his education or the kind of work he wants to do, he quickly decides to enroll in a college located in an area with the best weather or take the job that is closest to home."

"So, this race is about acting without thinking."

"It's usually unhelpful to go fast without first being clear on the direction we are going."

"You've got it. When we act without thinking about our values or thinking about the potential consequences, we often make decisions that don't help us. Like I said, it's not always bad to go fast. But it's usually unhelpful to go fast without first being clear on the direction we are going."

"Well, I'm glad to know it's okay to go fast."

Tortoise smiled. "I figured that would be a relief. Remember, we've updated our slogan."

Hare smiled in return. "It's really hard for me to imagine a tortoise acting impulsively."

"Oh, you would be surprised. I've certainly made some impulsive decisions in my day. It's important not to confuse going slow with being thoughtful or intentional. I've met some animals who get so overwhelmed that they don't move at all. Anxiety makes it difficult for them to decide on a course of action. Not moving at all or moving very slowly may be the opposite of impulsivity, but both lead to the same outcome: a disoriented, unsatisfied life."

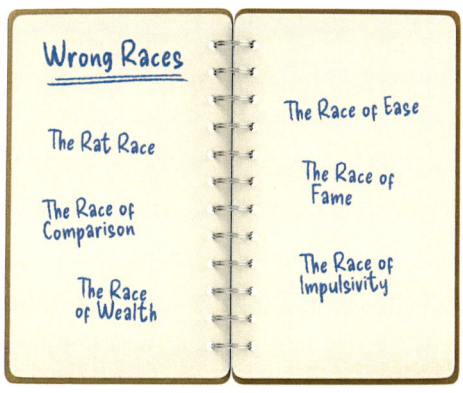

Wrong Races

The Rat Race

The Race of Comparison

The Race of Wealth

The Race of Ease

The Race of Fame

The Race of Impulsivity

"Are there other ways we act impulsively?"

"We give up too quickly."

Hare looked down, his expression suddenly sad. "I know that one a little too well."

"Yes, we all do. It can be hard to make commitments, but it can be even harder to keep them. When we're trying to make changes, we're likely going to encounter obstacles and discomfort. The question is, can we keep trying and not listen to the thought that tells us to 'give up'? And that's going to be important to consider as we move into learning about the right races. As you start running the right races, there will be times when you want to give up. The key is to avoid acting on that impulse and keep running."

Hare took a deep breath and looked at his notes. "Wow!" he said. "That's a lot of wrong races we run. Let me make sure I have them all." He read aloud. "Here are the six unhelpful races we run:

1.   The Rat Race
2.   The Race of Comparison
3.   The Race of Wealth
4.   The Race of Ease
5.   The Race of Fame, and
6.   The Race of Impulsivity.

Now that we have these, is it time to CHOOSE the PLAN?"

"Almost."

"Almost?" gasped Hare.

"Yes. We've reviewed a lot today. I'm thinking that this could be a good time to take a break from the action and end here for today. What do you think?"

"Well, I don't love that. But I guess it's important that I don't act on my impulses!" He sat back in his chair and after some thought said, "In fact, to demonstrate my commitment to change, I'd suggest we get back together in one week. That will give me some time to think about these races and prepare myself to CHOOSE the PLAN. Will that work for you?"

"Sure. Sounds great." Tortoise replied as he led Hare outside. "Have a great evening, Hare. I look forward to seeing you in a week."

CHAPTER EIGHT

CHOOSE THE PLAN

Hare eagerly anticipated his next meeting with Tortoise. He slightly regretted asking for one week between lessons. It felt like a very long time. But he also knew it was important that he practice patience.

So, he woke up bright and early the day of their meeting. He felt excited and hopeful. He was ready to CHOOSE the PLAN, whatever that meant. After a quick breakfast, he picked up his notebook and pen, placed them in his backpack, slid it over his shoulders, and hopped to Tortoise's house. The bright sunlight reflected off the morning dew. At times, it made it difficult for him to see, and yet it seemed that this was the clearest day he had had in his life.

As soon as Hare knocked on Tortoise's door, it swung open. A very cheerful Tortoise greeted him with a warm hello and a steaming cup of coffee. "Good morning, Hare! Come on in."

"Good morning, Tortoise. I will," answered Hare as he stepped inside.

"Are you ready to CHOOSE the PLAN?"

"You bet! I could hardly sleep, I was so excited."

"I love the anticipation." said Tortoise as he motioned him to have a seat. Hare sat down, removed the notebook and pen from his backpack, set them on a nearby stand, and took the cup of coffee Tortoise handed him. "And I see you have your notes."

"Yup. Let's do this!"

Tortoise stepped into the kitchen briefly to grab his own cup of coffee, sat down and began. "CHOOSE the PLAN is an acronym for ten lessons that will help you win in life. We'll start off with the PLAN, review each of the four lessons one at a time and discuss an action step you can take to live out each of them. The lessons are:

"**P** for Pursue your purpose"

"**L** for Love consistently"

"**A** for Act intentionally"

"**N** for Notice the positive."

Tortoise paused briefly so Hare could finish writing out the acronym and the words each letter stood for. Then he continued. "We previously discussed the wrong races that we run. The PLAN consists of the four right races to run. There are, of course, more than just four right races to run in life, but these four races, the Race of Purpose, the Race of Love, the Race of Action and the Race of Noticing the Positive are races that, when run well, contribute to a satisfying life. When we're clear on our purpose, loving others consistently, noticing the positives in our life and taking actions aligned with our values, we are taking the steps needed to win in life.

"Next, to run these four races well and ultimately win in life, we need to develop skills that create inner strength. CHOOSE consists of six lessons that promote adaptability, optimism, mindfulness and resilience in our lives. They are:

C for "Control the process."
H for "Hold on to hope."
O for "Observe your thoughts."
O for "Open up to fear."
S for "Sustain your efforts."
E for "Embrace the race."

Tortoise added, "The acronym is CHOOSE the PLAN, but we start with PLAN. This might seem backwards, but it's intentional. We start with PLAN because the "P" stands for "Pursue your purpose," and our purpose is the foundation of winning in life."

Hare wrote them down and then reviewed the ten lessons. "It's a bit frightening to start with purpose since I have no idea what my purpose is."

"Yes, it can be scary to talk about purpose. It's a BIG idea. But we purposefully start with purpose," said Tortoise with a smile. "Do you like that repetitive sound?"

Hare chuckled as Tortoise continued. "We start with purpose because clarifying it is like having a compass. When we are clear about what matters the most to us, it can guide all of our decisions, choices and actions. Purpose gives us direction and meaning."

Hare nodded. "The Plan starts with purpose. That makes sense to me."

"Good. So, let's start with an easy question," said Tortoise. "What's your purpose?"

Hare raised his eyes and retorted, "That's not such an easy question."

Tortoise smiled and took another sip of coffee. "Yes, I'm just kidding. It certainly is not an easy question. It isn't easy to identify what your purpose is, especially if you haven't been thinking about it. It's more helpful to think about it this way: What do you value? What do you care about most deeply?"

Hare considered Tortoise's questions. "It's hard to say. That's part of my problem, I guess. It feels like I've been living without direction. I'm like our poor hamster friends on a hamster wheel. I'm moving, but I'm not going anywhere. I think I've been living the six wrong races you talked about, and I'm starting to realize none of those are helpful." Hare paused. "Do you know what your values are, Tortoise?"

*"Purpose gives us
direction and meaning."*

"Some of my values have changed over the years, depending on my life circumstances. The truth is it has taken me quite a while and lots of mistakes or dead ends to identify my purpose. But today I have a good sense of what values to live by. They include being kind to and spending time with my wife and friends, doing my best at work, and remembering to thank God for all the good things I have. I try to live a life of generosity, creativity and service. When I think about the values that are most important to me, I've discovered that my purpose is to help others live the life they were created to live."

"Those are great values and a great purpose. Can I just steal yours?" They both laughed. Then Hare shook his head in frustration and asked, "How do I find out what I value?"

"That's a great question. But, before I tell you a good way to discover your values, let me make an important point about them. Your most meaningful values will always involve others."

———

"It's not about you, it's about who you can help."

———

"How so?"

"It's easy to become focused on values that only involve ourselves, like running the races of wealth and fame. Like we discussed last week, the problem with those values is that they don't last and aren't fulfilling. It's funny that we all seem to want these things, but they are never satisfying. The animals and people who have these things often seem the unhappiest. One's true values will always involve serving others. You can think of it this way: It's not about you, it's about who you can help. Ask yourself, 'Who can I help with my gifts and strengths?'"

Hare repeated, "*It's not about you, it's about who you can help*. That makes sense. I've spent a lot of time trying to impress the other animals. And no matter how much I impress them, it's never enough. You are right. It's never satisfying." He shook his head as though trying to get it to work better. "Okay, so back to my question. How do I figure out what I value?"

Tortoise handed Hare a piece of paper with the following 30 values.

Adventure	Family	Humor
Beauty	Fitness	Justice
Challenge	Friendship	Knowledge
Compassion	Fun	Love
Contribution	Generosity	Mastery
Creativity	Gratitude	Mindfulness
Curiosity	Growth	Relationships
Duty	Health	Service
Ecology	Hope	Simplicity
Faith	Humility	Work[1]

"Here are 30 values that are important to a lot of animals and even humans. What I want you to do is choose the ten values from this list that you feel are most important."

Hare scanned the list. "These all sound important. I can only choose ten?"

"Yes, only ten."

Hare took several minutes to review the list. "Okay. Here are my ten values: Adventure, Compassion, Contribution, Creativity, Faith, Friendship, Fitness, Generosity, Gratitude, Love and Mastery."

"Hey, Hare, that's eleven, not ten."

"I know. I was hoping you weren't counting!"

The friends laughed together. Tortoise looked Hare in the eye. "Well then, you're not going to like the second part of this activity."

"There's a second part?"

"Yes. Now, from the list of eleven values, choose the five most important values."

"I can only choose five?"

"Yup."

Hare spent a long time selecting his values. "Okay, here are the five I chose: Adventure, Contribution, Faith, Friendship and Gratitude. Wow, that was tough!"

"Yes, it is a tough exercise," Tortoise replied. "Of course, a short exercise like this one isn't going to provide us with absolute clarity on our values. And that list of 30 values isn't meant to be exhaustive. But it can be a helpful starting point. You now have some clarity on what matters most to you. So, let's summarize what you've learned from the exercise. At this moment in time, CHOOSE the PLAN means living a life that is full of adventure, contributes to others, lives out faith, and is full of friendships and gratitude. That's your list, right?"

"It is. And I like it!" Hare exclaimed. "I like it a lot!"

"Cool. Well, this is probably a good place to stop. I mentioned that the first four lessons each have an assignment. So, here's today's assignment. For your five values, I want you to identify a specific action you can take over the next week that puts the value into practice."

"How so?" Hare felt a little overwhelmed again.

"One of my values is service. I can live out that value by asking my wife how I can help her today."

"I get it. Thanks for the clarification." Hare grabbed his pen, wrote out the day's lesson, 'Pursue your purpose,' and then drew a compass to remind him that his values provide him with direction. He put down his pen and asked, "So, when can we meet again?"

"Let's plan for one week. That will give you time to do things that are examples of those values in action."

"Okay. Sounds good." Hare grabbed his notebook and pen and put them away. He gave his friend a fist bump and then hopped out of the house. He turned around as he was leaving, "Thanks, Tortoise! See you in one week."

CHAPTER NINE

LOVE
CONSISTENTLY

The week passed quickly. Hare felt like he was on a roller coaster. Having more clarity about his purpose and values was exciting, but in other moments, he felt overwhelmed. He realized how often he didn't live out his values, so he vacillated between moments of excitement and discouragement. He reflected on these thoughts as he made the short trip to Tortoise's home.

As on previous days, Tortoise welcomed him immediately with a friendly "Hey, Hare, how's it going?" and a cup of coffee.

Hare was tempted to say everything was fine, but he decided to be honest. "Up and down," he said in a subdued tone as he stepped inside the door, slipped off his backpack and took the coffee. The two friends sat in their accustomed chairs and placed their cups on the coffee table.

"That's a common experience," said Tortoise compassionately. "How did the assignment go?"

"Well, I wrote down something specific I could do for each value." Hare pulled his notebook out of the backpack and read his list. "They are:

- **Adventure**: Run through the forest and zipline myself from one tree to the next.

   That was fun. It was challenging to zipline without having opposable thumbs, but I figured it out!

- **Contribution**: Help out another animal in need.

   I didn't do that one. I didn't even know where to start.

- **Faith**: Go to church.

   I didn't do that one. I didn't want to see the other animals. I was afraid they might tease me.

- **Friendship**: Reach out to a friend and talk with them.

   I spoke with Beaver, who lives in a nearby river. It was good talking with him.

- **Gratitude**: Write down something I'm grateful for.

   I didn't do this one. It was hard for me to figure out what I'm grateful for.

"So, I acted on some of my values, but not all of them. And I didn't live them out as often as I would have liked to."

   Tortoise nodded. "It's not easy living out our values. Some days it comes naturally, and some days it feels nearly impossible. We're going to talk about some different ways to navigate those tough days effectively.

"But before we do that, we need to finish up the PLAN. Today, we'll focus on the 'L' that stands for 'love consistently.' Now when I'm talking about love, I'm not just talking about someone's love for a spouse, significant other or for one's kids. More generally, I'm talking about treating others with kindness and respect in order to develop strong and meaningful relationships."

———

> *"A winning life is never lived in isolation. The most fulfilled people have meaningful lives that are defined by strong, healthy relationships."*

———

Hare leaned back in his chair with an attentive look on his face, and Tortoise continued. "A famous human said, 'At the end of the day, it's not about what you have or even what you've accomplished; it's about who you've lifted up and who you've made better. It's about what you've given back.'[2] A winning life is never lived in isolation. The most fulfilled people have meaningful lives that are defined by strong, healthy relationships. We sometimes have the belief that we don't need any help, that we can figure life out by ourselves. But without connection and the support of others, we typically feel lonely and isolated."

"I agree with that," said Hare. "I thought I could do life by myself. In doing so, I tended to push others away. Now I'm starting to realize just how important relationships are."

"They are important, and our relationships won't flourish unless we prioritize them." Tortoise got out of his chair and quickly—as quickly as tortoises can move—went into his bedroom. He returned holding a piggy bank that he handed to Hare.

Hare shook the piggy bank. "Umm, it sounds empty. I was hoping you were giving me money. So, what is this for?"

"It's a bank I've had since childhood, but I keep it as a reminder. I want you to imagine that everyone has a piggy bank. Every day we have a decision to make. Will we deposit something in someone else's bank, or will we take something from it? When we encourage, uplift and inspire someone, we deposit in their bank. When we criticize or nag, we withdraw from their bank. Some of the most unhappy animals you'll encounter are those who have empty banks."

Hare grimaced. "I don't think I've done such a good job depositing in anyone's bank. I've probably done a lot more withdrawing."

"It's certainly easier to withdraw than deposit," acknowledged Tortoise. "But here's the thing: When we deposit in another animal's bank, we experience a deposit of positivity in return. On the other hand, when we withdraw from anyone's bank, we experience a loss of positivity."

"You're saying that when we give positivity to others, we usually get it back?"

"Yup! When you smile at someone, it's amazing how often they smile back." Tortoise looked out the window and then asked, "Would you be up for a walk? I want to show you something."

"Sure!"

The two friends got up, opened the door and walked out into the forest. It was mid fall, and the trees were a mass of different colors. Tortoise led them down a winding path for a few minutes without saying anything. Then he began to point out all the yellows, browns, pinks, reds and shades of green that adorned the leaves. Hare was amazed by the rich colors. He had never taken the time to pay attention to the natural beauty that surrounded him. *"It's like a masterpiece,"* he thought. *"It's more beautiful than anything an artist could create."*

Tortoise seemed to read Hare's mind, "Beautiful, right?"

"It sure is."

"You know what's interesting? In a month or two these trees will be pretty ugly. They will be bare. The beautiful colors will be replaced by monotonous shades of gray. Certainly not a pleasant prospect," he observed.

"But," he added quite emphatically, "when we see those empty branches, we know that they won't be empty for too long. Even in the depths of winter, we know that spring is coming. Green buds will start to form. The leaves will slowly return as suddenly the forest comes alive again!" Hare smiled at the thought.

"So, Hare, my question for you is, can you see the beauty in others? Much like barren branches eventually become vibrant with leaves, can you see the potential in others? Can you see what they can become? And can you encourage, coach and help them succeed?

Hare's eyes widened. "Other animals often live up to or down to our expectations of them," Tortoise noted. "We win in life when we see the potential in others and deposit encouragement in their piggy banks. That's why it's important to surround yourself with those who encourage you."

Hare suddenly realized that Tortoise saw his potential even though he viewed himself as a barren branch. "Tortoise, I'll never be able to thank you enough for your support. Thank you for depositing kindness and encouragement in my piggy bank. When I came to your house after the race, I felt like a completely barren branch. But you didn't see it that way. Somehow you saw the potential in me, and through your encouragement and wisdom, I can now see myself coming alive. I'll never be able to repay you."

> ## *"Can you see the potential in others? Can you see what they can become?"*

"Thanks, Hare. But it's not about repaying. It's about giving. And part of giving is the willingness to support and encourage others consistently, even when they are annoying or frustrating. It can be challenging to love, support and treat others with kindness when they are acting unkindly to us. We can all at times be unpredictable and imperfect in our interactions. But when we are willing to be gracious, forgive, and treat others with generosity, we are loving consistently, and in return we receive connection and positivity. I am more able to treat you well because others have treated me well.

"And now you can give that same gift to someone else. I am certain that at some point in the near future an animal is going to come to you and ask for your help. They will notice the change in you and see your hope and optimism. That will be your opportunity to give back, and when you seize that opportunity, you will find that their piggy bank is overflowing and you will feel great as well."

Tortoise and Hare took one more appreciative look at the leaves. Then Tortoise said, "I don't know about you, but I'm feeling a little cold. Let's head back to my house."

The two friends walked back to Tortoise's house in silence, each reflecting on their earlier conversation. When they arrived, Tortoise opened the door for Hare and they stepped inside. They sat down in their usual seats, and Hare smiled as he took out his notebook, placed it on the coffee table in front of him, and wrote, "Love consistently: Fill the piggy bank." He drew a piggy bank and a tree full of leaves to remind him to view others positively. "I think I know the answer to this, but what's the assignment for 'Love consistently?'"

"As you might guess, it's to look for an opportunity to praise and encourage someone else."

Hare wrote down the assignment and said, "Tortoise, you're a great teacher. Does that count for my assignment?"

"No, that's a little too easy." Tortoise smiled. "But thank you anyway."

Hare sighed in pretended disappointment. "I guess I'll have to encourage another animal."

Tortoise chuckled. "It will be good practice," he said. "Well, that's the lesson of 'Love consistently.' This is probably a good place to end for today. When we meet again, we will move on to the 'A,' Act intentionally. And let's plan to meet in two weeks. That will give you a little extra time to focus on supporting and encouraging others."

"I'm okay with that. I'd like to see you sooner, but I think two weeks makes sense. Thanks again, Tortoise."

"My pleasure, Hare. Keep up the great work! I'll see you then."

CHAPTER TEN

ACT INTENTIONALLY

The two weeks went by quickly, and as before, Hare experienced some ups and downs. There were moments when he was able to live out his values by encouraging his friends, and that felt good, but as time passed, a negative mindset seemed to dominate. He began to feel discouraged, wondering if he was ever going to be able to CHOOSE the PLAN consistently. As he approached Tortoise's door and knocked, he thought, "*Why am I even bothering with this? I'm just going to fail anyway.*" The door swung open, briefly interrupting his negative thoughts. He tried to hide his sadness, but it was too late.

"Hi, Hare. Come on in. You're looking a little down. What's going on?"

"Oh. Um. I don't feel like I'm doing a great job choosing the PLAN. I feel like such a screw-up. I'm just wasting your time."

"Whoa. Your mind is getting you pretty good."

"Yes, I guess so."

"Well, that's not a problem. I'm sure today's lesson will help lift your spirits."

"I hope so."

Tortoise and Hare took their usual seats in the living room. Hare laid his backpack on the floor by his chair as Tortoise leaned forward. "Since we've talked about pursuing your purpose and loving consistently, it's time to talk about acting intentionally."

With some reservation, Hare took out his notebook and wrote "Act intentionally."

"And to take action, we have to 'get off our buts.'"[3]

Hare smiled. "Get off our butts? Okay, I'm intrigued."

"Well, first let me clarify. It's 'get off our B-U-T-S.'"

"Now I'm even more intrigued!" said Hare and chuckled.

"It's very easy to create reasons or excuses. For example, tell me what happened to you this week? Were you able to live out your values and encourage others?"

Hare gulped. "Well, at the start, yes. But as the two weeks went on, not so much."

"Why not?"

"I wanted to reach out to my new neighbor, but then I thought that I always seem to say the wrong thing. So I didn't say anything to him at all. Then I started to feel bad, and when I felt bad, it was hard to be adventurous and grateful."

"So, you wanted to talk with your new neighbor, but you didn't because you were worried you would say the wrong thing. And you wanted to be adventurous, but you felt too bad to do so. And you wanted to be grateful, but you felt too sad to be grateful. Is that right?"

"Yes."

"Those reasons are really just 'buts.' And what happens when you listen to those 'but' thoughts?"

"Nothing good. I end up feeling down and unhappy."

"Our minds are terrific at creating reasons and excuses. Getting off our 'buts' means taking responsibility for our life and choosing to take actions consistent with our values, rather than allowing 'buts' and excuses to control our life."

"I like it, but how do I get 'off my buts?'"

"First of all, by changing your 'buts' to 'ands.'"

"Tell me more."

"'Getting off our buts' means taking responsibility for our life and choosing to take actions consistent with our values."

"All right, let's take your example of talking with your new neighbor. Your mind told you, 'I want to reach out to my new neighbor, but I always say the wrong thing.' You could change that to an 'and' by saying, 'I think I might say the wrong thing, AND I'm still going to reach out.' Changing from 'but' to 'and' is a skill that needs to be practiced repeatedly. It's a very important skill, because as you practice, it then allows you to create a plan of action."

"Hmmm, that makes sense. But what would a plan of action be?" Hare asked.

"It's about creating specific steps that lead you toward a goal you have. For example, if you want to talk to your neighbor, you could plan what you want to say, practice it and then make the commitment to do it. Choosing the PLAN is all about taking action. The PLAN is useless without action. You have to choose to act consistent with your purpose and values. Our 'buts' often represent the greatest barrier to taking positive action."

"I can see that now."

"Good. Success and fulfillment don't happen on their own. They happen when you live out your purpose consistently. They happen from actively engaging in your relationships. They happen when we act. Unfortunately, our minds are better at coming up with reasons to avoid action than helping us do something. That's why it's so important to turn those 'buts' into 'ands.'"

"All right, so what's my assignment?"

"It's creating an action plan for one of your values. Here are the five steps you need to take. Are you ready to write them down?"

"Yup!"

"Okay. I'll pause between each one to give you time to write.

Step 1: My value is _____

Step 2: My goal consistent with my value is _____

Step 3: The smaller actions to achieve this goal are _____

Step 4: The first action I am willing to commit to is _____

Step 5: I will complete this first action on _____
(day, date and time)[4]

Those are the five steps. Got them?"

Hare wrote as quickly as he could, added the last period and sat back with a sigh. "Got it."

"All right. Why don't I give you a few minutes, and let you create your action plan?"

Hare thought for a little while and started writing.

Step 1: My value is friendship.

Step 2: My goal is to create new friendships with animals in the forest. Rather than trying to compete with the other animals, my goal is to develop relationships where we support and encourage one another.

Step 3: The actions required to achieve this goal are:
   a) I will ask my new neighbor if he needs any help with his new home.
   b) I will join a volunteer club that helps animals in need. This will be an opportunity to make new friends.
   c) I will focus on listening more and talking less when I'm speaking with another animal.

Step 4: The first action I am willing to commit to is asking my new neighbor if he needs any help with his home.

Step 5: I will ask my neighbor tomorrow before 5 p.m.

He then handed his notebook to Tortoise. "How does that look?"

Tortoise read through the steps carefully. "That's great! I love it," he exclaimed enthusiastically.

Hare smiled at his friend's encouragement. Tortoise handed the notebook back and said, "That's the end of today's lesson. What if we get back together in two weeks for the last lesson of the PLAN?"

"That sounds good, but before I leave, I want to write down one more thing to help me remember this lesson." Hare then wrote 'AND' in large, bold letters next to 'Act Intentionally,' to help him remember to change his 'buts' to 'ands.' He then placed his pen and notebook into his backpack and stood up. As he hopped toward the door, he said, "Thanks for today's lesson. I'm now ready to take action on my values. See you in two weeks." Tortoise waved good-bye as Hare quickly hopped out of sight.

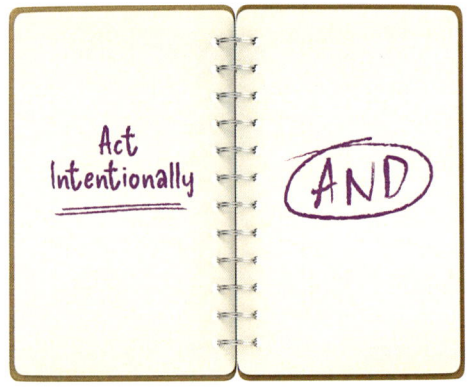

CHAPTER ELEVEN

NOTICE THE POSITIVE

Hare was pleased with the progress he had made. Although he knew there was still much to be learned, he was eager to share with Tortoise that he followed through with his action plan and asked his new neighbor if he needed any help settling into his home. His neighbor responded positively, and Hare spent three days helping him with his house projects.

On the day of their next lesson, Hare hopped quickly to Tortoise's house.

"Hi, Hare. You sure seem to be in a good mood," Tortoise observed as Hare almost knocked him over on entering the door.

"Yup. I followed through with my commitment and asked my neighbor if he needed any help. It turns out he did. It felt great to help another animal out!"

"Well, your positivity fits perfectly with our discussion today, because as you may recall from your list, the final lesson in PLAN is 'Notice the positive." I like to think of this lesson as, 'Give thanks for your shell.'"

"What? Give thanks for your shell?" Hare asked, a bit astonished.

"Yes, give thanks for your shell. How does that sound?"

"Um, honestly, it sounds goofy. I don't have a shell! You're going to have to explain what you mean."

"Well, my friend, you must first remember that a tortoise is sharing CHOOSE the PLAN with you. Obviously, hares don't have shells, so you can think of it as a figure of speech. Second, it's not easy being a tortoise. We tortoises are unusual. We are one of the slowest creatures and one of only a few animals that have a shell. We are unique, and I used to hate being so different. Let's just say, we are never chosen first for the sports teams."

They both laughed. "Yes," Hare said, "I get that, but after the other animals saw you beat me in a race, they might choose you first."

"I still doubt that," Tortoise answered, laughing again. "Anyway, I didn't appreciate what I had. I hated being slow, and I hated my shell. I judged my life based on what I didn't have. I envied your speed; I envied the deer's beauty and gracefulness; I envied the bird's flight; and I even envied the ant's strength. I compared myself to all the other animals, and I wanted to be a different animal. Do you ever feel that way?"

Hare shook his head in amazement. Tortoise had felt just like he had, except it was about different things. "All the time. It's funny, you envy my speed, and I envy the speed of the gazelle. I have always envied the intelligence of the elephant, and I also envy the peacock's beautiful feathers. I'm surprised you felt like I do."

"I did," replied Tortoise. "Then something changed for me. It changed when I learned this gratitude exercise, 'Write down three things you're grateful for every day.'[5] Of course, they can include things you have observed or experienced."

Hare pulled his pen and notebook out of the backpack and wrote the following: "Notice the positive. Write down three things I'm grateful for every day." He looked at his friend. "That sounds kind of challenging."

"It was hard at first. I didn't want to because it seemed silly to me. It felt too unrealistic. But I 'got off my buts' and did it anyway. At first, I would write down simple things, like 'I'm grateful that I have a job.' But the more I completed the exercise, the more aware I became of all the things I'm grateful for—including my shell."

"Really?"

"You bet. As I continued to write down my three gratitude statements, I became more aware of my blessings and over time my blessings grew. I no longer focused on the things I didn't have or the skills I lacked. It didn't matter that I wasn't as fast as a hare or as beautiful as a peacock. What mattered was that I became a more grateful tortoise and appreciated all of life more fully.

"I became more aware of my blessings and over time my blessings grew."

"I even realized that although my shell makes me stand out, it also protects me. It's one of the reasons why we tortoises can live until we are 100 years old."

"It sounds nice, but how do I do it?"

"Let's practice."

"Practice?"

"Yes, practice. Right now, tell me three things that you are grateful for today."

"Hmm." Hare squinted his eyes slightly and slowly thumped his leg as he attempted to identify three gratitude statements.

"I'm grateful that I'm spending time with you; I'm grateful for the sunshine; and I'm grateful for carrots."

"Because it's easier to focus on the negatives, we have to see the positives and practice being grateful intentionally."

"That's great, Hare. You did it!"

"I sure did. That wasn't as hard as I thought."

"Yes. And with practice, you might even begin to express gratitude for things you wouldn't have expected to, even for things like losing a race to a tortoise."

"That's just crazy talk, my friend."

"I know it sounds crazy, but think about it this way. It was only because you lost the race that you started to consider a different way of living. If you had won the race, you would have celebrated and nothing in your life would have changed. You'll find that with enough practice at expressing gratitude, you can learn to be thankful even during life's disappointments.

"We must search for and uncover the areas of life for which we are grateful. Because it's easier to focus on the negatives, we have to see the positives and practice being grateful."

"Wow, that makes a lot of sense. So, from now on I'm going to write down three things I'm grateful for every night."

"Good, because that's the assignment for this lesson!"

Hare smiled, and then looked quizzically at Tortoise. "So, what three things are you grateful for today?"

"Hmm. I'm thankful for our friendship; I'm grateful for my lovely wife; and I'm grateful for the smell of that delicious lunch coming from the kitchen. Would you like to stay for lunch?"

"Thanks for asking, but it's probably time for me to get going. I've got a lot to focus on this week. I need to keep getting off my 'buts,' take action and practice noticing the positive moments in my life. And I am up to the challenge!" Hare returned his attention to his notebook and drew a picture of a shell next to 'Notice the positive.' Hare placed the notebook and pen in his backpack, then stood up and gave Tortoise a fist bump. "See you in a week?"

"I was going to talk to you about that. The holidays are coming, and things are going to be a bit busy for us the next few weeks. How would you feel about taking a few weeks off and starting back up after the new year?"

Hare smiled ever so slightly. "Well, I'm not prepared to say I'm grateful for the break! But, ... I mean AND," Hare nodded playfully at his ability to change the "but" to "and," "it seems like this could be a good place to take a break. You've taught me the PLAN, and we can start off the new year with you teaching me how to CHOOSE." Hare leaned over, picked up his backpack and walked toward the door. Then he paused and turned back one more time. "Happy Holidays, Tortoise. I look forward to seeing you next year!"

CHAPTER TWELVE

CONTROL
THE PROCESS

Hare awoke the morning of their first meeting of the new year with a smile on his face. It had been a good few weeks. He had taken actions consistent with his values and practiced writing down his gratitude statements every day. Slowly but surely, he was beginning to notice more positives in his life, and as a result, he was feeling better about life and himself. As he made his way to Tortoise's house, he even wondered if he needed the CHOOSE lessons, since he was doing so well running the races of Purpose, Love, Action and Positivity. But he figured there was a reason Tortoise was going to teach him the CHOOSE lessons, and he certainly wasn't going to end the lessons early.

His thoughts turned from reflecting on the upcoming lessons to his excitement about reporting his progress to his friend. When he arrived at Tortoise's house, he walked up to the door to knock, but before he even touched it, the door swung open.

"Hi, Hare. Happy New Year! How's it going?" Tortoise asked cheerily.

Hare jumped back a little. "I didn't expect that!" he said with a laugh. "Actually, the last few weeks were pretty good. I've been doing much better at living out the PLAN, and I'm ready to start the new year by learning to CHOOSE."

"Excellent. I want to hear all about it. But can we walk and talk? For today's lesson, I think we should go for a swim."

"You want us to go for a swim? You do realize it's January! The water is probably cold, maybe even frozen."

"You're right. I'm not going for a swim; *you're* going for a swim."

"Huh? I'm going for a swim?"

"I appreciate your enthusiasm. Yes, you're going for a swim," Tortoise replied as he grabbed a few towels from the hallway closet, a wetsuit and a life jacket, which he handed to Hare.

Hare shrugged his shoulders, put the items into his backpack and followed his friend through the forest. As they walked toward the river, Hare told Tortoise about his successes from the past weeks. "I joined a volunteer club. We focus on helping keep the forest clean. As I was preparing to contact someone about joining the club, my mind 'but-ed' me: *'But you always say the wrong thing. It's a bad idea to join a club with other animals. You're just going to embarrass yourself.'* I changed that 'but' to an 'and,' and joined the club anyway. We had our first meeting, and I had a good time. And I also jotted down the three things I was grateful for every day."

"That's great, Hare."

"Yes, it sure is!"

When they arrived at the river, Tortoise said, "You have now learned the PLAN. When you live out your purpose, love consistently, take actions consistent with your purpose and notice the positive, you have what you need to win in life. But—and I do mean 'but'—sometimes our worries, doubts, thoughts and feelings can interfere with our well-being. We can get stuck in a negative mindset and end up feeling depressed and anxious. The acronym CHOOSE stands for six lessons that will teach you how to develop the inner strength to master those worries and negative feelings."

Hare took off his backpack, set it on the ground and squared his shoulders. "I am ready for CHOOSE," he stated confidently...and then paused. "But what does CHOOSE have to do with a swim in icy water?"

"The C stands for 'Control the process.' And to illustrate this lesson, I need you to jump into the river."

Hare grabbed his pen and notebook from the backpack, quickly scribbled, "Control the process," on a page, and returned the items to their place in the pack. He then put on the wetsuit and life jacket and jumped into the river. He bobbed a bit above the surface of the water since the life jacket kept him afloat. Tortoise watched Hare swim around for a couple of minutes and then motioned for him to come back to the bank. Hare dutifully swam to meet Tortoise, who reached out and placed a small rock on his back.

"Hey, what's that about?" Hare sputtered as he shook the rock off his back.

"Oh, that rock is *the expectations of others.*"

"Well, I don't really like that," said Hare as he spit out some water and continued paddling. After another couple of minutes, Tortoise asked Hare to swim back to him. Tortoise then placed a bigger rock on Hare's back. Hare shook the rock off his back vigorously.

"Hey!" Hare complained a little louder. "What's that?"

"Oh, those are *the negative thoughts and feelings of others*," Tortoise answered calmly.

Hare continued floating. About two minutes later, Tortoise asked Hare to meet him near the bank again. When Hare was within reach, he placed an even larger rock on his back.

Hare shook his body even harder, needing to exert more energy to free himself from the rock. "Okay, I'm not liking this lesson anymore!"

"That rock represents *your negative thoughts and feelings*," Tortoise stated as though it was a matter of fact.

"Well, my thoughts and feelings are saying that I don't want you to put any more rocks on my back."

Tortoise reached out and placed one more rock on Hare's back. "This is the last one. It represents *uncontrollable outcomes and events.*"

Hare started to sink slowly below the water. He paddled forcefully and shook himself free of the last rock. He then swam back to shore. "Phew. That was a scary lesson! Thank goodness those rocks can't stick to my back." he said as he stepped out of the river on to the muddy bank.

Hare removed the life jacket and wetsuit and shook some water off his fur. Tortoise handed his friend the towels to dry off and replied, "I know. And it's also scary. dangerous and even self-destructive when we try to change what we cannot control. When we burden ourselves with the uncontrollable, we begin to sink. We carry around the expectations of others; we strive to alter what others think, feel and do; we work hard to change what we think, feel and remember; and we try to control situations and events over which we have little influence. When we try to control things we have no power to modify or remove, we begin to feel overwhelmed and like we are drowning. The lesson is to let go of outcomes and control the process."

"It's scary. dangerous and even self-destructive when we try to change what we cannot control."

Hare repeated, "Let go of outcomes and control the process."

"That's right. It's exhausting to try to manage the impossible. I've spent a lot of time trying to change the negative opinions others had of me. I also exhausted myself trying to make my friends feel better when they seemed sad or anxious. And I was worrying all the time about results over which I had no control. I spent so much energy on impossibilities that I had none left to influence what I could actually modify or transform.

"I can't always control how others respond to me or their expectations of me, but I can control how I respond to others. I can't always change what I am thinking or feeling in the moment, but I can always control how I respond to my thoughts and feelings. When I stopped trying to control outcomes and focused more on the process, I stopped sinking in life. 'Control the process' means I take responsibility for my actions and focus on making the changes that create well-being in my life."

"Oh, I get it!" exclaimed Hare. "I have been so focused on trying to impress others and get them to view me as the fastest animal in the forest that I didn't focus on what I can control—things like practicing my running, keeping a steady pace, and not taking a nap during a race!"

"Exactly," said Tortoise. "I understand completely. In the past, I spent a lot of time trying to control what I was feeling. It can be scary being a tortoise. We're not the smallest, but we are definitely the slowest. So, in the past when I felt afraid, I felt weak. Then I started to beat myself up for feeling afraid. But the more I tried to stop feeling afraid, the more afraid I felt. By controlling the process, I now treat myself with more compassion. I remind myself that I'm going to have thoughts and feelings, and that at times I'm going to feel afraid. This kindness toward myself helps reduce my stress and increases my capacity for positivity.

"The definition of responsible is, 'able to respond.' We don't always choose what happens to us, but we can usually choose how we respond."

"On the other hand," Tortoise continued, "we can control how we respond to our thoughts and feelings. I have learned to think of it this way. The definition of responsible is, 'able to respond.' We don't always choose what happens to us, but we can usually choose how we respond. When we control the process, we can CHOOSE to live out our purpose, love others, take action and notice the positive."

Hare thought for a few moments about the lesson. It made sense to him, but he had one lingering question. "Does that mean we ignore outcomes?" he asked.

"Of course not, outcomes are still important!" replied Tortoise. "But we realize that we *influence* them; we don't control them. If we are getting results we don't like, we can alter the process and then see what changes. We are interested in the outcomes, but we are no longer defined by them."

"This lesson makes a lot of sense, and now,..." Hare stopped and shivered. "I am going to control this process. Can we please go back to your house? It's freezing outside and these towels aren't enough to warm me up."

"Of course!" Tortoise replied promptly. "That's enough of the outdoors for the day. What do you say we head back to my house, grab a warm cup of coffee, and do one more lesson?"

"Sounds great!"

CHAPTER THIRTEEN

HOLD ON
TO HOPE

The two friends walked back to Tortoise's home. Tortoise opened the door, and they walked into the sitting room. Fortunately, Tortoise's wife already had a pot of coffee brewing. "Anybody interested in a warm drink?" she asked with a smile.

"Oh yes!" they both chorused as they sat down. "Thank you."

She went to the kitchen and returned with two steaming cups of coffee. She handed one to her husband and the other to Hare. They thanked her again and sipped their coffee in silence for a few minutes.

"You warming up?" asked Tortoise.

"I sure am," answered Hare. "The coffee helps a lot."

"I'm sure it does," said Tortoise. "Are you ready for the next lesson?"

"Yup! Well, maybe I shouldn't answer so quickly. Does this lesson require me to jump into a river or do anything else crazy?"

"No. For this lesson, you don't even need to leave your chair."

"That's a relief!" Hare sighed. He then grabbed his notebook and turned back to the previous lesson, "Control the process." He realized he hadn't yet drawn an image for the lesson. After thinking for a few seconds, he drew a large rock next to the words. He placed his pen and notebook down on the table and looked at Tortoise. "Okay, I'm ready."

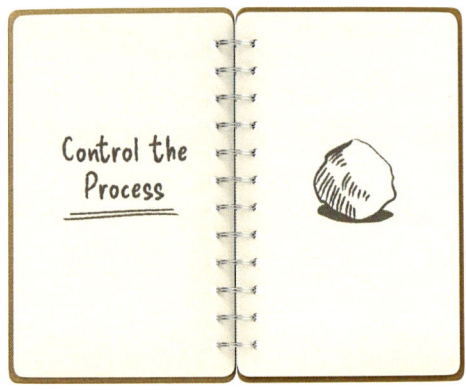

Tortoise began. "Very good. For this lesson, go ahead and close your eyes." Hare closed his eyes. "Good. What do you see?"

"I don't see anything."

"Nothing at all?"

"No. I just see darkness."

"No light?"

"Nope. No light."

"Okay. You can open your eyes."

Hare opened his eyes and gave his friend a puzzled look. "So, what's the lesson?"

"The lesson is, 'Hold on to hope.'"

"'Hold on to hope.' What does that have to do with closing your eyes and not seeing anything?"

"There are moments in life when things can feel pretty bleak. And there's no light at the end of the tunnel. In these moments, we often have the thought, '*It's always going to be this way. It's never going to get any better.*' At times like this, one of the most important values we can hold on to is hope."

"Yes. I know that feeling of hopelessness well. I felt that way after we had that big fire in the forest a few years ago." Tortoise nodded as Hare continued. "I lost everything I had. When the fire happened, I was scared and hopeless. I didn't think I'd be able to recover because of everything that I lost."

Tortoise nodded again. "We can't underestimate the power of hope. Life becomes most challenging when we lose hope. Here's what is important to remember. Hope isn't a feeling. It's a value. It's an action. It's what allows us to continue pursuing our goals and values even when it appears that our desired outcome is unlikely to occur."

Hare thought a moment before responding. "After I lost the race, I felt sad and lost. Walking to your house and asking for your help was one of the hardest things I've ever done. I did it because I hoped you could help me. And it turns out it was one of the best things I've ever done." Hare looked over at his friend and asked, "What does hope mean to you?"

"It used to mean I felt something. But now hope means the ability to take action in moments of doubt and uncertainty."

"Can you say more?"

"I'm learning that hope is the ability to see beyond the current circumstances, beyond my current feelings. Sometimes our emotions can be so powerful. When I'm feeling discouraged or depressed, it seems like that feeling will last forever, and it's easy to give up and stop trying. To hope means being able to see that there can be positive changes in the future, and then taking positive actions that are consistent with your purpose, even if you're doubting that those actions will make a difference."

> *"I'm learning that hope is the ability to see beyond the current circumstances, beyond my current feelings."*

Hare agreed. "It can be hard to hope when we're feeling overwhelmed."

"Right. And that's why hope is an action. Not every day is perfect, and I still experience some hard days. But my days are also filled with gratitude, joy and meaning. And these days come from the ability to hold on to hope even when it's hard, from the willingness to take another step even when I'm scared, even when I'm doubtful."

"So, hope allows you to see the light at the end of the tunnel?"

"I think it's even more than that. Hope allows you to keep taking steps toward your goals even when it's dark. It's knowing that the difficult emotions won't last forever even though it feels like they will."

"That is hard."

"Yes, it is! It's easy to hope when things are going well. But when circumstances are against us, it's difficult. And that's also when hope becomes very important. Because when you are hopeless, you stop moving and you stop growing."

"What can I do in those dark moments?"

"It's not usually helpful to fight against them. That can make the dark moments even darker. But what can be helpful is to remember that previous dark moments haven't lasted forever. Our thoughts, emotions and circumstances are constantly changing."

"Yeah, that's true."

Tortoise paused again and then said, "Let me explain this with an example. Do you like the winter?"

"Not particularly. I don't like the cold, and I don't like swimming in icy water."

"Me either. This shell I have isn't insulated! But what helps me navigate the winter is the realization that winter doesn't last forever. I know, based on my experience, that spring eventually comes.

"Hope allows you to keep taking steps toward your goals even when it's dark. It's knowing that the difficult emotions won't last forever even though it feels like they will."

"Yes, that's true."

"Now, here's the important point. If it's wintertime and you think you can't live your life fully until the spring comes, that's a recipe for hopelessness. We aren't bears. We don't hibernate. While we're waiting for spring, it's important to continue living out our purpose, continue to live out love, continue to take meaningful actions, and continue to live out positivity. In many ways, holding on to hope looks like continuing to live out the PLAN even if it doesn't feel like it's making a difference. Doing so can actually make spring come a bit sooner!"

"So, I don't have to wait and see if the groundhog sees his shadow?" asked Hare.

Tortoise laughed. "Nope. You don't need to wait for the groundhog to have hope."

"That's good to know! Let me make sure I'm understanding this. 'Hold on to hope' means not letting the hard moments determine my actions. There are going to be times when I CHOOSE the PLAN, and life will feel great. But there are other moments when I'll experience sadness and discouragement. 'Hold on to hope' means sticking with the PLAN during those difficult moments."

"You got it! You said that better than I did."

Hare picked his pen and notebook up from the table and took a moment to write out the lesson's title, "Hold on to hope." He drew a sun next to the lesson to remind him that hope is knowing that spring will come even when we're in winter's dreariness. Hare placed the pen and notebook into his backpack and said good-bye to Tortoise. Little did he know that soon he'd have the chance to put the lesson into practice.

CHAPTER FOURTEEN

OBSERVE YOUR THOUGHTS

The day before Hare's next meeting with Tortoise, he was taking a hop through the forest, noticing many things for which he was grateful and enjoying the pure white snow weighting down the branches when he encountered his nemesis, the Skunk. *"Oh no! Not Skunk! He stinks!"* Hare thought. He tried to hop the other way, but it was too late. Skunk had spotted him.

"Well, well, well. How's it going, slowpoke?" Skunk sneered.

Hare felt a whirlwind of emotions rush through his body. He had no love for Skunk and no interest in viewing him as a barren tree branch that would one day bloom. His thoughts raced. His body tensed. He didn't want to act impulsively, but before he knew it, he blurted out, "Oh shut up, Skunk. No one wants to hear you. You're such a jerk."

"Whoa. What's wrong with you? I'm just trying to say hello. Although I can understand why you're a little on edge. You did, after all...." Skunk trailed off as he started to laugh. "You did, after all, lose a race to a tortoise!"

As Skunk bellowed with laughter, Hare became even angrier. His thoughts were spinning out of control, and his paws were clenched. He shouted, "It could have happened to any hare!"

"Ha. Losing a race to a tortoise? No, that couldn't have happened to any hare. That could only happen to you—though I've got to give you credit. If I had lost to a tortoise, I wouldn't be walking in the forest. I would be hiding in my hole. It's impressive that you are willing to be seen outside." The sarcasm dripped from the skunk's lips.

Hare felt like he was going to burst. His heart was racing, and his vision narrowed. Skunk's words were fighting words. However, before Hare could respond any further, Skunk brushed past him with a parting shot. "So long, chump. You might think that I smell, but you've got the smell of loser all over you."

Hare stood silent. He felt embarrassed, angry and guilty all at once. *"How could I let Skunk make me so upset? I thought I was doing better than that."* Hare paced through the forest for another hour, imagining all the different ways he could have responded to Skunk. He replayed the conversation over and over. Finally, exhausted, he dragged himself home. He was disappointed in himself and felt defeated. "I'll never learn the lessons Tortoise is trying to teach me. Maybe Skunk is right; I am a loser," he said out loud to no one in particular.

The day slowly turned to evening. He climbed into bed and wrestled with his thoughts. He was grateful that he would see Tortoise in the morning, but also felt embarrassed that he would need to report his failure. He tossed and turned as he replayed his interaction with Skunk.

When the morning sun began to rise, Hare crawled out of bed, wiping the sleep from his eyes. He was fatigued and grumpy. He left his house and did a few double takes, making sure Skunk wasn't waiting to make his life miserable again. His walk to Tortoise's house seemed to take forever. He was weighed down by "I-should-have" and "I'm-not-good-enough" thoughts.

Finally, Hare arrived and knocked on the door slowly. He was greeted with an enthusiastic, "Hi there, buddy!" Then Tortoise noticed his friend's sad expression. "Hey, what's wrong?"

Hare stood in the doorway with sagging shoulders. "I'm never going to learn how to do this. I'm never going to CHOOSE the PLAN. I failed you. You should stop teaching me."

Tortoise stepped back to let Hare come into the living room. He walked in and slumped into a chair. Tortoise walked over to his chair, sat down and leaned toward Hare. "Hmm. You've been practicing hard and making a lot of progress. What happened?"

"Do you know Skunk?"

Tortoise nodded. "I don't really know him. But I know of him."

"Well, I saw him in the forest yesterday when I was taking a walk. I had been doing so well living the PLAN. I was taking a few moments to notice some of the beauty around me. And then I see him in the forest, and instead of leaving me alone, he insults me. He makes fun of me for losing the race to you. He's such an idiot."

"Then what happened?"

"Well, I was just so mad. I called him a jerk and was ready to fight him. But before I could do anything else, he left. I was thinking about it all day. It makes me mad that he made me so angry. What's wrong with me?"

"There's nothing wrong with you," Tortoise said reassuringly. "In fact, your interaction with Skunk provides the perfect example for our next lesson, 'Observe your thoughts.'"

Hare's eyebrows rose. Tortoise then walked over to the window. He pulled back the shades and commented, "Look at that! It's snowing!"

"Snowing? Ugh. Isn't winter over yet? And it isn't even supposed to snow today. I looked at the forecast before I left. Cold and clear was the prediction."

Tortoise chuckled as snowflakes floated to the ground. "I guess the prediction was wrong."

Hare sighed. "Yes, that often seems to be the case."

"Weather forecasters are always making predictions, and they are sometimes wrong. The same is true of our thoughts. Our thoughts are constantly making predictions, and they are often wrong."

"How so?"

"Think of all the negative thoughts you've experienced that don't come true:

What if they don't like me?
What if I fail?
What if something bad happens to me?
What if I get bad news about a family member's health?

Sometimes our thoughts are accurate. But more often than not, they are inaccurate."

"I guess so," Hare said quietly.

"I did some research to determine what percentage of thoughts are negative. What do you think I found?"

"I don't know," answered Hare and thought about his experience. "I guess maybe 50%."

"One study I read found that nearly 80% of our thoughts are negative."[6]

"Eighty percent? Wow, that's a lot!"

"It sure is," Tortoise agreed. "And it means that you're not alone in experiencing negative thoughts, thoughts that tell you, you are a loser or that something is wrong with you. It turns out we all have those thoughts. Some of the negative thoughts are about ourselves, some of them about others, and some about the world."

"Why do we experience so many negative thoughts?"

"Because the purpose of our thoughts is to protect us. Our thoughts try to keep us away from pain and danger. Good things don't represent danger, so they don't stick with us. But negative experiences represent pain, so our thoughts tend to dwell on the negative to protect us from danger."

Hare's eyebrows rose again.

"Let me give you an example. Have you ever taken a test and only missed one or two questions?"

Hare nodded.

"And what did you focus on?"

"The one or two questions I got wrong."

"Exactly. And you're not alone in that. Most of us do the same. And we do this because the purpose of our thoughts is to keep us safe, to help us look for danger and prevent loss, injury or death. But that's also why it's so important that we remember how many of the weather forecaster's predictions are inaccurate. If thoughts aren't facts, it means that we don't always have to listen to our thoughts. When our thoughts are filling us with negative predictions, we can acknowledge that our thoughts are trying to protect us, but we don't have to listen to them."

Hare repeated, "Thoughts aren't facts." He then frowned ever so slightly.

"Something bothering you?" asked Tortoise.

"I guess I disagree a bit. I do agree that most negative thoughts tend to be false or inaccurate. And it's nice to know that 80% of thoughts are negative. It helps me not feel so crazy. But here's my problem: sometimes my thoughts do turn out to be true. For example, one of the scariest thoughts I had before racing you was, 'What if I lose to a tortoise? That would be horrible.' And I did lose to a tortoise!"

"Thoughts aren't facts. When our thoughts are filling us with negative predictions, we can acknowledge that our thoughts are trying to protect us, but we don't have to listen to them."

"Yes, that's a good point. And that's where we turn to our trusty friend, the spider."

"The spider! What can we learn from a spider?" Hare asked.

"Have you ever hopped into a spider web?"

Hare laughed. 'Yes, I have experience with spider webs. I've accidentally run into a few, and they are so sticky. What a weird feeling." Hare shook his body as he remembered the sensation.

"Yes, they sure are. And here is the lesson we can learn from our spider friends:

'Just as spiders catch their prey in their webs, we can catch the thoughts in our minds.'"

"Catch our thoughts? What do you mean?"

"When we experience negative thoughts, often our tendency is to try to push them away, fight them, distract from them, or just avoid them. But this can make the thoughts worse. On the other hand, we can choose to catch them by saying to ourselves, '*I'm having a thought*,' or simply saying, '*Thanks, mind*.'[7] Once they are caught, we can decide if the thought is helpful or unhelpful. If the thought is helpful, we can pay attention to it and listen to what it is telling us. If the thought is unhelpful, we can acknowledge it, leave it in the sticky goo, and go on to live out our purpose and values."

"*We can catch the thoughts in our minds.*'"

"Hmmm. What's an example of a helpful thought?" asked Hare.

"Several weeks ago, I was walking through the forest when I heard some branches move. I paused for a moment and took several more steps. Suddenly, I heard that high-pitched, unmistakable coyote howl. I'm not sure if you know this, but we tortoises aren't real big fans of coyotes. Immediately I had the thought, '*Danger. I've got to get to safety!*' As quickly as I could, I found cover and shrank into my shell. In that moment, the thought, '*You're in trouble, get to safety*,' was very helpful."

"Okay. That makes sense to me."

"Here's why this is important," explained Tortoise. "Thoughts aren't always facts, but they can still be scary because sometimes thoughts do turn out to be true. The lesson of the spider web reminds us that what matters isn't whether the thought is true; what matters is whether the thought is helpful.

"When my thoughts told me, *I'm super slow and I'm going to lose the race to the hare,*' they felt quite true in the moment. BUT they weren't helpful, so I chose not to listen to them, and I kept running."

> **"What matters isn't whether the thought is true; what matters is whether the thought is helpful."**

"W-well," Hare stammered. "I'm now thinking about the race, and it's so embarrassing. I see so clearly how and why I lost. When I got my big lead, I had the thought, *I am the best! That tortoise is so slow that he'll never catch up to me.*' I didn't realize it at the time, but even though they were positive thoughts, they were also very unhelpful. I sure wish I hadn't listened to them. It was silly for me to have those thoughts."

Tortoise gave Hare a compassionate look. "My friend, we've all had moments when we listened to unhelpful thoughts. And hey, one more thing to notice: When you said, 'It was silly for me to have those thoughts,' that's a thought, too, and an unhelpful one at that."

Hare chuckled. "Yeah, you're right. Wow, this catching thoughts thing isn't so easy!"

"No, it's not. If you keep practicing, you'll continue to get better at it. But here's one thing to remember. There are some thoughts that are often more difficult to catch than others. In my experience, the most difficult ones to catch are a variation of, 'I'm not good enough.'"

Hare's heart skipped a beat and his stomach tightened. He didn't want to admit it, but he often struggled with thoughts of not being good enough. His voice quieted. "Yeah. That is, ummm, well. Yeah, I have those thoughts. I often feel like I'm not smart enough."

"Those thoughts can be hard. They can cut to our core. But here's the hope. When we can start catching those thoughts, too, we spend a lot less time trying to prove our worth, and a lot more time living the PLAN."

"Yeah, that sounds good."

Tortoise looked at his friend, "Well, I think that's all for today. Keep choosing the PLAN and catch those thoughts."

"I sure will!" Hare quickly grabbed his book and pen from his backpack and wrote the day's lesson, "Observe your thoughts." He drew a spider web next to the lesson. He returned the book and pen to his backpack, got up, and stepped to the door. "Thanks for today's lesson. I really needed it. See you in two weeks." Hare hopped away from his friend's house, excited to continue practicing what he was learning.

CHAPTER FIFTEEN

OPEN UP TO FEAR

Hare worked hard to capture his thoughts with decent success. However, he found some thoughts, particularly thoughts related to fear, difficult to catch. Every time he walked through the forest, he dreaded encountering Skunk again. The last few days before meeting with Tortoise, he took fewer walks in the forest in the hopes that he wouldn't run into him.

Tortoise had touched base with him and asked if they could meet at Hare's house for the next lesson, so he was sitting in his front room with his feet propped on a stool awaiting his friend's arrival. Hare was thinking about the previous lesson when a few light taps sounded on the door. He jumped up and opened it.

"Hi, Tortoise." he said. "Come on in. It's good to see you. How are you?"

"Pretty good," Tortoise replied as he stepped inside. "How about you?

How has thought-catching gone?"

"Not bad. I definitely was able to catch many of the thoughts like, '*I'm not good enough*.' It helped me feel less bogged down. But there were certain thoughts I struggled to catch."

"Which thoughts were those?"

"I was convinced that I was going to see Skunk in the forest again. It felt like more than a thought. It felt real. So, I took fewer walks in the forest."

"Ahh."

"Ahh?"

"Yes, that's perfect."

"That's perfect?"

"Yes. A perfect example for today's lesson," Tortoise explained.

"So, what's the lesson?"

"Let's take another walk," proposed Tortoise. "There's something else I want to show you."

The two friends left Hare's house, and Tortoise led him to a nearby swamp. Hare's nose twitched in disgust as they neared the murky water. "*No wonder I stay away from here*," he thought. "*It stinks*."

Tortoise, however, had other things in mind. "We can learn a lesson from this swamp.[8] Here we are, standing on solid ground. This represents what you know. It represents your comfort zone. Because it's known to you, it can feel pretty safe." Tortoise then pointed to a small body of land jutting out of the water in the middle of the swamp. Sunlight filtered through the trees and lit it up.

"Do you see that little island in the middle of the swamp?"

"Yes."

"That land represents what you want your life to be about. It represents the values and purpose you identified in the PLAN. And in between your comfort zone and the PLAN is this stinky, scary swamp. You look into the swamp while standing on the solid ground that you know, and you're quite sure you see these scary creatures. The swamp is muddy, dirty and unknown.

---

*"Fear is a part of you,
but it doesn't define you."*

"It feels so much easier to just stay in your comfort zone and play it safe, thinking to yourself, *'I'll jump into the swamp when I feel a little more confident, when the swamp isn't so dirty.'* But it's a swamp. It's never going to be completely clean. However, there's a cost to staying in our comfort zone. We lose out on what matters most to us. We don't live out our values. So, the question is, are you willing to take a risk and wade through the swamp in pursuit of what matters most to you? Are you willing to experience the fear and still choose the PLAN?"

"You bet I am!" And before Tortoise could blink, Hare had jumped into the swamp.

"Hare!" Tortoise yelled. "It was just an example to illustrate something really difficult. I didn't mean for you to actually jump in the swamp!"

"Ha! I know, Tortoise. But I wanted to show you that I could do it." Hare waded in the swamp for a minute and then paddled his way out of it. His snow-white fur had changed to a muddy dark brown. He shook himself thoroughly to clean off, nearly hitting Tortoise with dirty swamp water. He looked at Tortoise. "Yes, I am afraid. I'm afraid of failing. I'm afraid of running into Skunk again. I'm afraid of embarrassing myself. I'm afraid that others will reject me. I'm afraid of being vulnerable and ultimately getting hurt." Hare paused and then exclaimed, "I'm going to feel that fear, and I'm going to CHOOSE the PLAN even when I feel afraid."

"I love it! Fear isn't the enemy. Fear is a part of you, but it doesn't define you. In fact, none of your thoughts and feelings are the enemy. You can have your difficult thoughts and feelings, acknowledge them, and still go wading in the swamp."

Tortoise continued. "When we start living and swim in the swamp toward what is important to us, it can bring meaning and joy. There is something invigorating when we do something we care about even though it's scary. But when we avoid doing what's most important to us because we're afraid, life can feel boring, dull and heavy. So, when we wait to live, we add 'weight' to our lives."

"I like that," Hare said thoughtfully. "When we wait to live, we add 'weight' to our lives."

"When we wait to live, we add 'weight' to our lives."

Hare continued talking as the two friends started walking back to his home. "I don't want to add any more 'weight' to my life. There are going to be a lot of swamps that I encounter, and I look forward to wading through some of them."

"Yes. Fear and anxiety can teach us something. Sometimes the things that we're afraid of tell us about what matters most to us."

"Really? That's confusing. I'm scared of eagles swooping down and eating me, and I wouldn't say eagles matter to me."

"Yes, that's a good point! But in other situations, your fear might teach you about what's most important to you. You mentioned that you were scared to ask for my help. Why?"

"Because I was afraid you would be mad at me and tell me you couldn't help me."

"Exactly. You were afraid because you care about relationships, and you want to have meaningful connections in your life."

"I never thought of it that way."

"Right. When you notice anxiety or fear showing up, you can ask yourself, '*What might this be teaching me about my purpose and my values?*' Instead of being an enemy, anxiety and fear can then be teachers. And it's from this realization that we are better able to wade in the swamp and do what matters to us. When we open up to fear, we can then run the races of purpose, love, action and positivity. But, if we aren't willing to open up to fear, there's no opportunity to live out the PLAN."

Hare stopped for a moment and sat down on a nearby tree stump. He reached into his backpack, took out his notebook and pen, and wrote, "Open up to fear." He drew a little swamp next to the lesson. He then put the pen and notebook back into the backpack and resumed walking.

Tortoise continued. "If we think about purpose, love and action, these all involve experiencing some fear. If you live out a meaningful purpose that involves serving others, there are going to be more skunk encounters in your life. To truly love requires the willingness to be vulnerable, which is SCARY. And almost any time we are trying something new, it scares us. There is no PLAN without some fear. They are related."

Hare nodded his head in agreement though he felt a wave of anxiety at the thought of facing Skunk again. "I think it was probably easier wading into the actual swamp than it will be wading into the proverbial swamp of fear. But...," Hare squared his shoulders, "I mean... **and** one of the first things I'm going to do to face my fear is take a walk in the forest, even if I do see Skunk."

"That's great to hear." Tortoise said as he fist-bumped his friend. "And I actually have one more opportunity for you to open up to fear."

"You do?" asked Hare a bit hesitantly. "What is it?"

"You and I should run a rematch. What do you think?"

"A rematch?" Hare nearly screamed.

"You bet. It's the perfect event for you to apply the skills you've been learning."

"Uh, I'm not sure what to say."

"Well, that's different," said Tortoise with a smile, and they both chuckled.

Hare thought for a few moments. "Well, that does sound kind of fun. When would we do it?"

"How about in eight weeks? We'll start the spring season with a race."

"Yeah. That gives me enough time to practice all of the skills we've learned so that I'm ready."

Hare stopped walking and became so distracted by thoughts about the rematch that he didn't hear Tortoise calling his name.

"Hare. Hare. HARE!"

"Oh, sorry, Tortoise. You just caught me off guard with that rematch talk."

"No problem, friend. I'm sure there are lots of thoughts for you to catch. Do you think that you're up for one more lesson today?"

"Um, yeah, I guess so. That might actually be helpful. Maybe it will help me focus on something besides all these anxious thoughts."

"Okay. Follow me."

CHAPTER SIXTEEN

Sustain Your Efforts

Tortoise led Hare to a stream that cut through the forest. Tortoise sat down near the bank of the stream, and Hare followed his lead. Tortoise then pointed to the rocks that were scattered through the stream bed. "Take a look at those rocks. Many of them were much bigger many, many years ago. But the consistent flow of the stream has slowly changed their size and shape. Someone once said, 'Over time, a slow, steady stream of water will erode the hardest rock and turn giant boulders into pebbles.'[9]

"And that leads us to our next lesson, 'Sustain your efforts.'"

Hare's ears perked up as he grabbed his pen and notebook and wrote, "Sustain your efforts." "For a moment, I thought you were going to tell me the lesson was, 'Slow and steady wins the race.'"

Tortoise laughed. "No, like I said, we've updated our marketing! But it's still helpful to consider the importance of consistent effort. Life can be good at throwing us curve balls. One of the important skills we can develop is being resilient."

"What do you mean by resilient?"

"I mean you consistently take actions defined by your values and directed toward achieving your goals, even when facing obstacles. We are fascinated by the overnight success story, the rags to riches. But the truth is, very little success happens overnight. Success comes from consistent effort, from persistence and perseverance. That means doing what you need to do even when you don't want to do it."

"Success comes from consistent effort, from persistence and perseverance."

"That doesn't sound like fun."

"Sometimes it's not. Sometimes it's challenging and really hard! But let's think about the alternative. The alternative is jumping from one idea to the next idea and then the next. Or jumping from one goal to the next goal and then the next. Or jumping from one relationship to the next relationship and on to the next. Or sometimes we settle for only making small goals for ourselves to ensure we don't experience obstacles and challenges. Do you know anyone like that?"

Hare looked away uncomfortably. "Yeah, me."

"And how has that worked for you?"

Hare straightened up. "Well, not too well."

Tortoise asked. "What have you found as you've jumped from one idea to the next?"

"I feel excited in the moment, but the excitement fades quickly. And it never leads to any sustained success."

"That's right!" Tortoise stated emphatically. "It can be difficult to be resilient, but when we don't choose to keep going in life, we're often left feeling disappointed and discouraged because we don't accomplish our goals."

"I agree. But how can I sustain my efforts?"

Tortoise smiled. "I'm glad you asked," he said. "Sustaining your efforts starts with the recognition that some days almost everything goes well, and some days are filled with challenges. We begin telling ourselves, '*I shouldn't feel tired. I shouldn't feel discouraged. I shouldn't have a bad day.*" But when we do this, we cause ourselves frustration and guilt. We begin beating ourselves up, which can create a self-fulfilling prophecy and cause us to have more challenging days."

"I can relate to that. But I thought we're always supposed to give 100%?"

"Yes, it's important to give 100% of what you have that day. If you're at 80%, give 100% of 80%.[10] When we believe we have to be perfect every day, we exhaust ourselves and might end up stopping, burning out or never starting. Instead of focusing on being perfect, 'sustain your efforts' allows us to recognize that progress is more important than perfection. As long as we're consistently working on our goals and living out our values, we're making progress, even if we're not achieving those goals as quickly as we'd like to."

"Progress is more important than perfection. That's a relief," sighed Hare.

"It sure is. And it's also important to remember that life isn't a competition. 'Sustain your efforts' means staying in our lane, and measuring our progress based on where we started, as opposed to measuring our progress compared to where someone else finished." Tortoise paused, looked his friend in the eyes and said, "And you can be proud of your achievements."

Hare looked confused. "Proud of my achievements? Why would I be proud? I still have so much to learn."

"You can be proud because of the progress you have made. You've shown up. You've opened up to fear. You've identified your purpose. Every day, you are 'embracing the race' by CHOOSING the PLAN."

"Progress is more important than perfection."

Hare considered his friend's words for a few minutes. For the first time in years, he felt a sense of achievement. He was proud, but ironically this pride came from a place of humility, of understanding the importance of being true to his values. There was no sense of cockiness. He had no desire to show off what he was learning. Instead of showing off to others, he began to notice a desire to share with others. For most of his life, he had felt out of control and aimless. He felt like his emotions had dictated everything that he did. But now he was beginning to feel like he could choose his actions. He had a sense of purpose, and he was living his purpose. He wasn't doing it perfectly, but that was okay. A little smile touched his lips.

Tortoise saw the smile. "Hey, I see that smile. What's it about?"

"I'm just grateful for everything that you're teaching me. It's nice to see the progress you've helped me make. Thank you."

"You're welcome. It's been great to see you apply these lessons. What do you think? Why don't we call it a day, and we'll finish the final lesson next week?"

"Sounds great!" Hare grabbed his notebook and pen, then paused a moment as he considered an appropriate illustration. "Got it," he said suddenly and drew an image of "100%" next to the lesson title.

After returning the pen and notebook to his backpack, he stood up and started running home, but suddenly slowed to a leisurely hop. He turned around, looked back at Tortoise and grinned. "Look at me," he said. "I'm walking instead of running. I'm sustaining my progress."

Tortoise laughed and waved, grateful to know that his friend was succeeding.

CHAPTER SEVENTEEN

Embrace
the Race

A mixture of emotions greeted Hare the morning of his final lesson. He was excited that his lessons were nearly over. He knew he had made great strides though it hadn't been easy. There had definitely been moments of failure. But he was much more able to hold on to hope, control the process, observe his thoughts, and in doing so he was able to live out the PLAN. And he was also sad. He knew his friendship with Tortoise would continue long after these lessons, but he would certainly miss the learning moments. The trip to Tortoise's house seemed extra short since his competing emotions distracted him.

When Hare got closer, he saw that Tortoise was waiting for him at the front door. "Hey, Hare! It's hard to believe today is our last lesson."

"I know. Where did the time go?"

"I don't know. What do you say we go for one more walk?" It was unseasonably warm for early spring, and Tortoise wanted to take advantage of the warmer temperatures, as well as use nature to provide one more teachable moment.

Hare looked up at the gray sky that seemed to be darkening by the minute. "I would love to, but that sky looks ominous."

Tortoise shrugged his shoulders. "That's why I have a shell to protect me from the rain. What do you say?"

"Uh, I don't have a shell, so I'll need an umbrella."

Tortoise laughed as he handed his friend an umbrella, and they then strolled down the path through the forest. They were only a few minutes into their walk when small raindrops started to fall. The rainfall quickly intensified, soon accompanied by lightning and thunder. Hare ran for cover under a tree and huddled under his umbrella. After a minute, he realized he was by himself. He looked around for Tortoise and found his friend jumping up and down in a puddle, splashing around like a kid. "Tortoise!" he yelled. "What are you doing?"

"I'm having fun! Come join me!" Tortoise shouted through the downpour, as he continued to jump and splash. After a few moments of indecision, Hare gave in to Tortoise's enthusiasm and jumped in a nearby puddle with a big splash.

Then the rain stopped as quickly as it had started. Hare and Tortoise laughed and jumped in the puddles for a few more minutes until they were finally worn out. Tortoise turned to his friend. "This reminds me of one of my favorite quotes: 'Life isn't about waiting for the storm to pass; it's about learning to dance in the rain.'"[11]

"That's a great quote."

"And it speaks to the last lesson, 'Embrace the race.' That's right, our new slogan is the last lesson. 'Embrace the race' means living life with purpose and not letting the negative moments in life defeat you. You will encounter challenges, obstacles and painful moments. But instead of giving up or running the wrong races, you can 'Embrace the race' and run the four races that lead to a successful, fulfilling life, the races of Purpose, Love, Action and Positivity. Was it annoying that it started raining and interfered with our walk? Absolutely. But instead of letting the negative moments define me, I want to embrace the moment, accept it as it is and keep taking action. Come on. I want to show you something."

"'Embrace the race' means living life with purpose and not letting the negative moments in life defeat you."

Tortoise scanned the horizon. The sun had started to peek through the clouds, and a vibrant rainbow could be seen in the distance. He motioned for Hare to follow him. "You probably don't know it," he said, "but the end of the rainbow touches down deep in this forest." Hare shook his head in bewilderment and followed Tortoise down a long path he had never seen before. After a very long walk, Tortoise stopped and pointed. "So, what do you see?"

"A rainbow touching the ground," Hare answered in amazement.

"And what do you see at the end of the rainbow?"

"Ummm. Nothing?" he replied hesitantly.

"Exactly. Nothing."

"So, what's the point?"

"Nothing is the point."

"There is no point?"

"No. Nothing is the point."

"I'm confused!"

Tortoise laughed. "Do you know the saying, 'There's a pot of gold at the end of the rainbow'?"

Hare nodded his head.

"Well, there's not. That doesn't mean we shouldn't be optimistic; it just means we shouldn't fool ourselves. There are no pots of gold, and there are no leprechauns at the end of the rainbow. And here's the point. We want things to happen quickly. We want to find the shortcuts. We're tempted to run the wrong races we discussed. But most of the time, success only comes through challenging moments. We need to embrace the challenging times and continue to live out the PLAN."

"I guess you're right," observed Hare. "I've been trying my whole life to find the shortcuts. But there aren't any shortcuts to living a purposeful life. Someone once said, 'It took me 25 years to become an overnight success.'[12] And I now agree with that. Has it been difficult at times for you to 'embrace the race' over the years?"

"I'm not perfect at the lessons and I never will be. But I've found that working hard to live them out consistently has helped me experience a life full of joy and meaning. Life isn't always easy, but I can honestly say that I love my life."

"You've sold me on 'Embrace the race.' It's very clear that there's no pot of gold at the end of the rainbow. I thought there was, and I'm now realizing how easy it is to become distracted by overnight success stories. It's obvious that those stories are the exception. You're teaching me that victory in life comes from running the right races, and not giving up when obstacles occur."

"Yes," Tortoise replied, "and speaking of races, have you been thinking much about our rematch?"

"Not much—just every waking moment."

The friends laughed. "You're not dreaming about it, too, are you?" Tortoise joked.

"When I cross the finish line in the rematch, I'll be a very different hare compared to when I crossed the finish line in our first race."

"No, it's not quite that intense. But I have been thinking about it. I'm nervous, but I'm ready. The more I think about it, the more I realize it's the perfect way to conclude the lessons. When I cross the finish line in the rematch, I'll be a very different hare compared to when I crossed the finish line in our first race."

"There is no doubt about that!"

Hare thought about the lessons that were coming to an end. His heart fluttered and his stomach tightened slightly. He swallowed and then looked at his friend, "Thanks again, Tortoise, for everything you have taught me. I am a different hare, an improved hare, because of you. I have so greatly enjoyed our time together. You've challenged me and encouraged me. Thank you for everything."

Tortoise gave Hare one final fist bump. "It's been my pleasure!"

"Well, if I'm doing my math correctly, it's seven weeks until our rematch. I'll see you then."

"Sounds good!"

Hare removed his notebook from his backpack, placed it on the ground, and wrote the title of the final lesson. Next to it he drew a pot of gold. He put his notebook back in his backpack and waved good-bye to his friend. They parted ways, both the better for the time they had spent together over the past several months.

CHAPTER EIGHTEEN

THE RACE

The seven weeks went quickly and slowly for Hare. As the day of the race drew closer, he was filled with excitement and anxiety. He was eager to see all the animals at the race and show them the changes he had made. But he didn't want to show them to get their approval or to boast. Instead, he wanted them to see that change was possible.

The day of the rematch finally arrived. Anticipation filled the brisk morning air in the clearing where the animals were gathering. They were all talking. A rematch between Hare and Tortoise? This was an event that had to be seen. The animals arrived early. And a few even made some funny signs: "Hare, we've got a hammock for you." and "Tortoise the Torpedo!"

When Tortoise and Hare walked into the clearing, the animals were surprised to see them together. They seemed friendly. Perhaps even more surprising, the hare appeared to be different. There was a new spring to his hop. He pointed to the "Hare, we've got a hammock for you," and laughed. He even went to the sign and autographed it.

The animals slowly began whispering to one another, "Hare seems different. What's going on with him? He seems a lot less annoying."

Hare turned to Tortoise. "Well, buddy, the race is here. I sure hope I don't trip or fall or get scooped up by an eagle!"

"And I hope I don't flip over on my shell. But I'm not too worried about eagles scooping me up. I don't think they are too fond of shells for dinner."

Tortoise gave his friend a fist bump. Hare then looked toward the starting line. "Well, it looks like it's about time to start the race. Let's go. See you at the finish line."

Hare and Tortoise walked to the starting line. Just as in their first race, Zebra officiated. He motioned for the animals to quiet down and began describing the course. "Tortoise and Hare, you'll start by running on the path through the middle of the forest. When you reach the Blue Diamond Pond, continue to your right. You'll run around the pond and then find a gravel path that the humans made. Take that path to the towering evergreen tree. Behind the evergreen tree, there is a dirt trail. Take that trail south, and it will bring you to the finish line. Any questions?"

Both contestants shook their heads, indicating that they understood.

"Okay, if there are no questions, I'll turn it over to Parrot!" The large Macaw had agreed to whistle loudly to signal the beginning of the race. Everyone held their breath and then instantly covered their ears when the Macaw once again screeched instead of whistling.

The race began, and Hare rushed out to an early lead. As he noticed his reflection in the pond, he thought, "*Just keep running the race. Catch those negative thoughts and embrace the race."*

Meanwhile Tortoise plodded methodically along the path and finally reached the pond. Much like the first race, he observed his reflection and thought, *"Just keep moving."* He felt tired and knew that Hare had a big lead in the race. *"Hare is going to win the race,"* he said to himself. *"I should just stop running."* But Tortoise caught his thoughts so that he could focus on enjoying the race and kept moving one step after another.

Hare made his way to the dirt trail. He was almost at the finish line, and the animals started to cheer. As he broke into a full sprint, he heard a cry come from the trees next to the trail. He came to a sudden stop. It sounded like someone was in pain. He looked toward the finish line, then into the trees. He didn't want to leave anyone hurting, but he wanted to win the race. He decided to take a few steps into the forest to investigate.

"Hello, is there someone there?" a frantic voice called. "Can you help me? I'm stuck. I hurt my foot, and I can't climb out! I need help!"

Hare recognized the voice. He took a few steps closer and confirmed his suspicion. It was Skunk. Somehow, he had gotten himself stuck in a hole and couldn't climb out. *"Ha!"* he thought. *"Looks like you got what's coming to you. Too bad, Skunk. If you had treated me better in the forest, I might have helped you. Payback stinks, doesn't it?"* He turned to start running the race again. There was no way he was going to help someone like him.

"Did Skunk deserve his help? Absolutely not. But it wasn't about whether Skunk deserved it. Hare realized this was the time to 'win the race.'"

Then he started to think about the lessons he had learned in CHOOSE the PLAN. Did Skunk deserve his help? Absolutely not. But it wasn't about whether Skunk deserved it. Hare realized this was the time to "embrace the race." This was an opportunity to run the races of Purpose, Love and Action. He wanted to leave Skunk and win the race, but he wasn't running the wrong races anymore. He was running the right races, and in doing so he was winning in life.

Hare looked out to the finish line at all the cheering animals and looked back at Skunk stuck in the hole. He took a few deep breaths, grabbed a long branch and ran back to the hole. He handed it down to Skunk. He tried to climb the branch several times, only to fall back down. As Skunk struggled to hold on to the limb, Hare knew that soon there would not be enough time to help Skunk and still win the race. But he was okay with that because he was choosing to "win the right race." Finally, very slowly and gingerly, Skunk climbed up the branch and out of the hole.

Back in the clearing, the animals were shocked. Hare had been so close to winning! They had seen him nearing the finish line. Why did he go into the forest? A few of them started the rumor that Hare was taking a nap again. Apparently, he hadn't changed.

Meanwhile, Tortoise continued his slow, steady pace. He had no idea that Hare was helping Skunk. One step after another, Tortoise continued and finally entered the dirt path. He could see and hear the other animals roaring. As he took a few more steps on the dirt path, he heard rustling from between the trees on the path. Suddenly, Hare emerged, assisting the injured skunk.

"Hare! What's going on?"

Before Hare could open his mouth, Skunk answered. "I got stuck in a hole and couldn't get out. I was terrified and started to scream. Hare heard me and came to my rescue."

"Hare, you're a hero!" exclaimed Tortoise.

Hare smiled and looked away sheepishly. "No, not a hero. Just living out the lessons you taught me."

Their conversation was interrupted by the shouts of the animals at the finish line. Tortoise had an idea. "Hare, you're the true winner of the race. Go ahead and cross the finish line first, and I'll help Skunk walk to the clearing."

Hare turned to Skunk, who nodded in agreement. "Okay. See you soon." He sprinted across the finish line while Tortoise assisted the hobbling skunk.

The animals initially gave Hare a mixed reception, uncertain of what had happened. Several of them congratulated him while others chattered quietly, obviously confused. A few minutes later, Tortoise and Skunk crossed the finish line.

> *"Hare smiled. 'Well, I won the race, but thanks to you I've won much more than that.'"*

Though clearly in pain, Skunk faced the crowd and explained, "I had run into the forest because I was planning to jump out at Hare and tease him. Well, there was a hole I didn't see, and I fell in, hurting my foot pretty badly. I couldn't get out. When I heard someone on the path, I yelled for help, and much to my surprise Hare came to the hole where I was. I can't believe he helped me after the mean things I said to him. He really has changed!"

When Skunk finished talking, the animals rushed over to Hare. They picked him up and started chanting, "Hare! Hare! Hare!"

Finally, after several minutes, the animals put Hare down. Tortoise made his way through the crowd to find Hare and yelled. "Hare, you won!"

Hare smiled "Well, I won the race, but thanks to you I've won much more than that."

"What made you decide to help Skunk?"

"The PLAN, of course."

Tortoise laughed.

"I thought about everything I've learned," Hare explained. "In that moment, it was more important to me to help Skunk than it was to cross the finish line first. So, I chose to 'embrace the race' and do what truly matters."

Hare took a deep breath and looked around at all the animals still talking and laughing in the clearing. "Wow, it has been quite the day. But I can tell you, I will never forget this moment. Thank you again for everything that you taught me. Today was an amazing day!"

"Yes, it was," Tortoise agreed. "And I'll never forget this day either. Well, I don't know about you, but I'm pretty tired. I think it's time to go home and get some rest."

"Sounds like a good idea. See you soon, my friend."

"Thanks, Hare. I'll see you soon."

CONCLUSION

We know that money can't buy happiness, but many of us work hard trying to prove that idea wrong. We understand that we can't make everyone like us, but some of us spend a lot of time seeking the approval of others. We know that fame is fleeting, but we work hard to be an influencer. It turns out that well-being is rarely found with a number: the number of likes we get on social media, the number of friend requests we have, our weight on a scale, the money in our bank account or the square footage of our house. All these numbers entice us to place our value in these very tangible, concrete outcomes. The problem is that they are fleeting, lacking and inconsequential. They lead us to run races that are unfulfilling or even harmful.

My hope is that *The Tortoise and the Hare Retold* will cause you to think differently about the races you're running. The risk of writing a book like this one, or more specifically in offering an acronym, such as CHOOSE the PLAN, is that it implies a simple equation leads to a winning life. It seems to say, "Follow these ten lessons, and you will always be happy!" Life, of course, never fits in a formula. As opposed to this book being the "Answer," my hope is that it will cause you to pause, think about and consider what matters most to you. I hope that after reading it you'll begin to experience your thoughts and feelings differently, that you won't view them as experiences that must be avoided. Furthermore, I trust that you'll prioritize your relationships, discover the beauty of positivity and hold on to hope.

Thanks for taking the time to read the book. In this fast-paced world, there are many activities that can attract your attention. Reading, in itself, may represent a more methodical, persistent effort. Many blessings as you "embrace the race" and CHOOSE the PLAN!

AUTHOR'S NOTE

I hope that you enjoyed reading *The Tortoise and the Hare Retold*. My goal was for the book to be playful and fun, while at the same time helping you grow and win in life. Just as importantly, the guidance offered throughout the story is evidenced-based and supported by empirical research.

The majority of the lessons come from two resources: acceptance and commitment therapy (ACT) and positive psychology. If you're interested in learning more about ACT or positive psychology, visit this book's website: *HighTidePress.org/tortoise*. There you will also find the resources and references that were used in each chapter.

ACKNOWLEDGMENTS

Writing a book often feels like a race. It's exciting to cross the finish line and see the finished product. But writing a book is not a solo race. It is much more like a relay, with many people running the race with me!

The first "relay runners" I'd like to thank are my friends at High Tide Press. Mary Rundell-Holmes is such a gifted editor and so much fun to work with. Many thanks to her for using her skills to add image and playfulness to the book. Anne Ward's enthusiasm and encouragement are inspiring and helped me keep writing in the challenging moments. Art Dykstra's wisdom, leadership and insights are unparalleled. I am so grateful for the conversations I had with Art about winning in life. They not only helped me write the book, they helped me experience more fulfillment in my life. I am grateful to Bob Sandidge for his tech-wizardry and to Beth Dyer for her kindness and support.

Another "runner" to whom I owe many thanks is my friend and mentor, Dr. Thane Dykstra. Thane is a tremendous leader and a true friend. He introduced me to both acceptance and commitment therapy (ACT) and positive psychology, and taught me to ask important questions. His positive influence has shaped my life and career forever. Thane exemplifies what it is to be a servant leader.

I could not have accomplished what I have as a psychologist and author without the support of my family members. They have provided that support in a variety of ways.

My brother Bob, his wife Georgann and their two precious girls, Lucia and Cecelia bring me constant happiness. I am so grateful for our closeness. And Bob ran a marathon while I was writing this book. I am very proud of him.

My mom is a constant source of encouragement. Her faith, passion for life, kindness, courage and love are a blessing. She has helped me keep running during the most challenging moments of my life. She exemplifies Christ's love in everything that she does. It is because of my mom and dad's hard work and sacrifice that I have the privilege of being a psychologist.

My wife Aimee is a true blessing. I love being married to a fellow "runner" in the field of psychology. Aimee's love and support fuel me every day. She brings me joy and meaning. I love running the race of life with her!

And Aimee and I love running this race of life with our children, Michael Antonio and Alivia. There is no greater blessing than being a parent. They have taught me how to see life through the eyes of a child, and I'm convinced that is the best way to live. They remind me to wonder, create, laugh, play and be silly.

My dad passed away while I was writing this book. He was kind, wise, thoughtful, generous, supportive, humble and gracious. He touched so many lives and was truly the best father anyone could ask for. I hope and pray that I can be the father to my children the way my dad was to Bob and me. We all lost when Dad passed away, but I truly believe that Dad ran the right races and won!

ENDNOTES

1. This values exercise is derived from the longer Personal Values Card Sort authored by William R. Miller, Janet C'de Baca, Daniel B. Matthews, Paula L. Wilbourne (Albuquerque: University of New Mexico, 2001).

2. Denzel Washington, *A Hand to Guide Me* (Des Moines, IA: Meredith Books, 2006), p. 23.

3. Steven C. Hayes, Kirk. D. Strosahl and Kelly G. Wilson, *Acceptance and Commitment Therapy: The Process and Practice of Mindful Change* (New York: The Guilford Press, 2012), pp. 262-264.

4. This action plan is derived from "The Willingness-and-Action Plan" created by Russ Harris in his book, *The Happiness Trap: How to Stop Struggling and Start Living* (Boston: Trumpeter Books, 2008), pp. 217-218.

5. Martin E.P. Seligman, *Flourish: A Visionary New Understanding of Happiness and Well-being* (New York: Free Press, 2011), p. 171.

6. NeuroGym Team, "New Study: You Have 6,200 Thoughts a Day...Don't Make Yours Negative." https://blog.myneurogym.com/new-study-you-have-6900-thoughts-a-day-dont-make-yours-negative.

7. Russ Harris, *The Happiness Trap: How to Stop Struggling and Start Living* (Boston: Trumpeter Books, 2008), pp. 92-93.

8. Steven C. Hayes, Kirk. D. Strosahl and Kelly G. Wilson, *Acceptance and Commitment Therapy: An Experiential Approach to Behavior Change* (New York: The Guilford Press, 1999), pp. 247-248.

9. Rick Warren, *The Purpose Driven Life: What on Earth Am I Here For?* (Grand Rapids, MI: Zondervan, 2002), p. 222.

10. Joshua Medcalf and Lucas Jadin, *Win in the Dark: Some think you shine under the bright lights, the bright lights only reveal your work in the dark* (Self-published, 2020), p. 115.

11. In addition to being used on a wide variety of decorative canvases and plaques, Vivian Greene's popular quote, "Life isn't about waiting for the storm to pass; it's about learning to dance in the rain," appears as the title of her address book, published in 2012.

12. This statement is a paraphrase of Dave Ramsey's Tweet, "I have worked my butt off for 25 years... now I am "An Overnight Success." 7:04 a.m., August 18, 2016.

ABOUT THE AUTHOR

Dr. Michael Mecozzi is a clinical psychologist, author and speaker. He and his wife, Dr. Aimee Echevarria, are founders of a private psychology practice, Hope with ME, in the southwest suburbs of Chicago.

He specializes in working with young adults and adults experiencing stress and anxiety. Dr. Mecozzi also created "RELAX," an interactive experience designed to help people master their anxiety so they can win in life. Dr. Mecozzi presents "RELAX" as a one-hour keynote or full-day workshop.

In his free time, Dr. Mecozzi enjoys exploring new adventures with his wife and their two young children.

If you're interested in working with Dr. Mecozzi or booking him as a speaker, he can be reached at drmecozzi@gmail.com. For further information, please visit his website: www.hopewithme.com.